SECRETS OF THE SUPEROPTIMIST

**A complete account of the original
116 wisdom transmissions.**

Witnessed and recorded by
W. R. Morton and Nathaniel Whitten

Cover: Stunt performer "Human Fireball" aka Louis T. Thunder dives into a water tank at the 1937 Minnesota State Fair. In 142 performances of this daring stunt over 10 years, Louis successfully entered the water without burns 95 times.

Image © Minnesota Historical Society/CORBIS

A
First Edition
Limited Printing
ISBN: 0-9774807-0-4
ISBN 13: 978-0-9774807-0-9

Vitally Important Books
www.vitallyimportant.com
SAN : 2 5 7 - 6 2 5 2

www.superoptimist.com
SUPEROPTIMIST™

GRATITUDE

The transmitters would like to express appreciation to all who helped during the process of bringing this book to life. Personal and individual thanks are due almost exclusively to the following: Marcy Sansolo, Jack Whitten, Dan Kennedy, Al Gore, Brother Benjamin, Sister Victoria, Jon Stewart, Billyweeds & Dolo, Big Ben and Lady Jane, Anne Morton, Chogham Trungpa, Tim Leary, Bill Murray, Fredericka Fairchild, Joey Joe Joseph, Wes Anderson, Dr. William Morton Jr., Andrea D'Aquino, Flea, Wayne Jones, Shaun Assael, Fred Paprin, Bill Bastone and thesmokinggun.com, Surie Cruise, Don Sheldon, Karina Fassett, David Statman, Ace Frehley, Bill Schaberg, Marke Rubenstein, Stevie H., Fred Schneider, Dr. Michler Bishop, Milton Haynes, Don "Swami of Grooviness" Perley, Cheetah Chrome, Martin Gardlin, Stuart "Uto" Whiteside, Dave Eggers, Hank Thoreau, J.D., Trudie Styler, Ellen Barkin, Dr. Robert Willis, Bill and Lois Wilson, Dr. Joe Gow, David Blaine, John, Tom, Jim, Dave, Chris aka The Mill River Band, "Big Daddy" Ed Roth, Eric Gregory, Michael Crichton, Hal Foster, Eric Blare, Scott Grieger, Tom Schoellhammer, Professor Ron Gottesman, H. Mark Roelofs, Carl Hiaasen, Andy Warhol, Dean Koontz, Andre Butler Parke, Richard Feynman, Kirstin Mac Dougall, Frank Ford, Theodora West, Alexis Smith, William Fordyce, William Cheung, Peter S. Gardos, Diane Sagnella, Don Ed Hardy, Barry Rothman, Sam Clemens, James Field, Jimmy Connors, Steven King, Charles Burns, Mary Tanner, Raymond Chandler, Maurizio Grimaldi, Stanley Kubrick, Douglas Allen, George Lucas, Sean McPhetridge, Michael Chabon, Jim Wedaa, Robert Heinlein, Mike MacNeill, Jennifer Joseph, Marc Gerald, Kem Nunn, Barak Kassar, Philip Owens, and of course, Sam and the Fiesta Brava restaurant crew.

Publisher's Note to First Edition

SuperOptimism is not to be confused with plain old ordinary optimism or other extropian principles, including the following: Utopianism, Intelligent Technology, Perpetual Progress, Self-Direction, Emotional Life Expansion, or Dynamic Tension.

The words contained within this volume are the result of a transmission from the Collective Sentience of Intergalactic Energy, transposed and codified by two human receptors for the benefit of all.

SECTION ONE

GENESIS OF THIS TEXT

The unconscious awakening which has resulted in the secrets you are about to read did not occur in a barren desert, or at the top of a mountain. Nor did it happen at the feet of a Tibetan sage or Zen master. We would tell you if it took place in a seminar, retreat, monastery, nunnery, or Quaker Meeting House. But it did not.

"Then where did it happen?" you might ask. As near as can be explained, it transpired in two suburban homes, over the course of the autumnal equinox, facilitated only by an unusual presence discovered to be living there, a presence that became known as The SuperOptimist.

While the no-mind reception of these "knowledge transmissions" may seem like a miraculous occurrence, they are in no way an unprecedented event.

Throughout history, every human culture has stories of ordinary individuals who were approached to record information by extraordinary sources. In most cases, the information was of unusual value and desperately needed by society at that point in time. Considering the vast tidepool of political disinformation, religious hysteria, and corporate malfeasance swirling in our midst, it is plain to see that this is such a time.

The individuals who have dutifully responded to the collection and dissemination of such wisdom have gone by many strange names, including: archimage, diviner, medicine man, seer, shaman, thaumaturge, magus, medium, occultist, mundunugu, obeah doctor, and wangateur. Even the grossly unfair "Ph.D." has been used in this regard, though often without substance.

In the case of SuperOptimism, the writing of this text began with episodes of "directed composition" where the transmitters of this work found themselves at their respective desks, one on the west coast of the Americas, one on the east. Naturally, both were wearing masks. (The shaman wears a mask to aid in communication with the "axis mundi," or spirit channel, between other planes of reality and Earth. This masked transmitter becomes a channel for a voice beyond our society.)

Shaman masks from around the world.

What are the odds that two men on opposite sides of a continent will simultaneously put on identical masks and begin writing the same text, with the same voice, as if they were one consciousness? In fact, this strange and mystical occurrence -- two minds acting as one from a distance of 3,085 miles -- has been deemed impossible by all known laws of physical science. So unlikely is this method of authorship that a noted mathematician at Santa Monica Community College specified odds of 185,766,453,230 to 1 *against*.

And yet, it did happen. The proof is in your hands. How? The explanation we favor is the following: communication was occurring on a superluminal spiritual channel, broadcast by The SuperOptimist and received by the recorders of this text as if they were satellite transponders with moveable appendages - poised over keyboards, ouija, pen, and paper.

Readers who find this explanation far-fetched may want to consider the latest scientific inquiry into the hidden 12-dimensional nature of the universe at a subatomic level. This inquiry tells us *for absolute certainty*, that there's more going on in the cosmos than we have direct sensory access to, and for good reason.

However, we don't need to know the inner thoughts of a quark, pi-meson, or gamma ray. And we wouldn't want to.

W.R. Morton & Nathaniel Whitten
Hotel Holt, Reykjavík 101, Iceland

METHODOLOGY

In the last few years, many people have inquired in various forums, meetings, and Q&A sessions about SuperOptimism and its categorization among Class 2 philosophies.

Questions include:

Is this a religion?
Is it a form of meditation?
Is it a program or school?
What does it cost?
How long does it take?

In reality, there is only one question absolutely essential to the pursuit of a SuperOptimistic outlook: *Are you prepared to change the way you perceive every person, object, situation, and animal in your life?*

Change is the hardest thing for a human being to face, and while SuperOptimism itself is not difficult, change, for most of us, is very difficult.

As a preparatory step towards this change, let's review a simple chart to help understand what is meant -- in broad terms -- by SuperOptimism.

In the *Figure 1 diagram* on the next page, you will see the mental states that are commonly experienced by human beings. They range from a state of despair to a state of joy. The "gates" to these opposites, joy and despair, are optimism and pessimism.

This lead us to the three working definitions which help us to better understand the significance of placing the word "Super" before the word "Optimist."

Optimist
One who usually expects a favorable outcome.

Pessimist
One who usually expects a negative outcome.

SuperOptimist
One who has learned the mental discipline to reframe any situation into a favorable outcome.

Therefore, we may extrapolate the following: If the situation is good, the SuperOptimist reframes it as "even better." If the situation seems bad, negative, gloomy, sad, doomed, or awful, then the SuperOptimist reframes that so-called "bad" situation into one that is just as "good" as a good situation. Or better.

PSYCHOGRAPHIC CHART OF
HUMAN EMOTION
&
MENTAL STATES

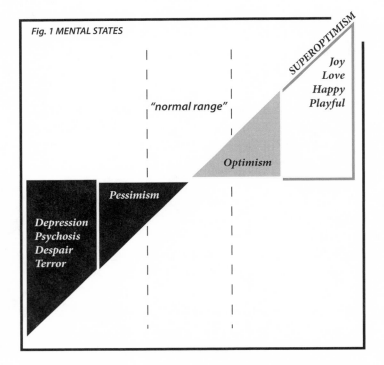

Fig. 1 MENTAL STATES

SUPEROPTIMISM

Joy
Love
Happy
Playful

"normal range"

Optimism

Pessimism

Depression
Psychosis
Despair
Terror

Psychologists identify human emotions as the following: anger, aversion, courage, dejection, desire, despair, fear, hate, hope, sadness, surprise, interest, wonder, sorrow, rage, terror, anxiety, joy, contempt, disgust, distress, guilt, shame, grief, elation, and love.

You may now ask, "How is it possible to turn any and all situations to the 'good'? Suppose I have a brand new car and a building falls on it and crushes it flat as a blueberry pancake. How can that be "good"?

It can be good because the car was not the best model for you.

It can be good because you can ride your bicycle for a few days and get some healthy exercise.

It can be good because this presents an opportunity for renewal and rebuilding on many fronts.

It can be good because you have a chance to get a ride with a friend or make a new friend.

Most of all, it can be good because you were *not in the car* when the building fell on it.

However, even if that were the case and you *were* in the car when it was crushed (which doesn't make much sense because you wouldn't be reading this book right now, but let's just say it did) then being in the car could be good because all your worries would be over, and you would be in a state of relative peace and would not have to worry about whether you paid your phone bill on time or not (also rent, gas, and electric.)

Sometimes it will seem very difficult to reframe an event (parking ticket, bad haircut, influenza, divorce) in a SuperOptimistic way, but fortunately for us, humans are very good at building habits into habitual behavior. Simply stated, if you can make a habit of being a SuperOptimist for 5 minutes today, you can be one for 10 minutes tomorrow, and 20 the next day.

To get started, we suggest reading these secrets in the order which they are presented. While some secrets will immediately resonate with you, others will undoubtedly require more study or will become more meaningful after you've grown comfortable with the introductory thought-reframing exercises.

Additionally, some find that throwing this book against a flat surface and reading from the open pages helps them focus on one secret at a time. Others close their eyes and open to a random page, absorbing the information that way. Still others place the book under their pillow at night, and are inspired by osmotic contact.

However you choose to utilize the secrets contained within, committing to a program of action is essential. Read, reframe, and *respond*. Most of all, congratulate yourself on beginning the journey down the magical hallway of SuperOptimism. You're well on your way to making your life the best it can be. And then even better than that.

IMPORTANT NOTES

Thoughtful readers have asked us the question: "Why are these secrets not numbered in sequential order?" Our reply is these secrets are accurately presented to you here exactly in the order of their transcription by the authors. The first secret written for this book was actually #115. Quite surprising, even to us. We believe the purpose of this seemingly random numbering is to encourage us to find our own personal meaning in our lives.

Many people have requested a "plan" of study to get them started on SuperOptimism. While excellent progress can be made with secrets chosen randomly, the following is one method that's been proven effective.

Suggested:

Secrets #115, #67, and #37

which follow directly.

SECRET #115

The luckiest human alive?
That's right, it's you!

With 298 million people in the United States, and an additional 6+ billion around the globe, you face long odds in anything you set out to accomplish: becoming a professional athlete, reaching the top of the corporate ladder, winning a $150 million PowerBall jackpot, finding a suitable life partner, beating Stage 4 lymphoma. If you stare hard at the statistics, you may wonder "what's the use" and give up before you even start.

Not the SuperOptimist. He simply balls up the actuarial table and moves forward, secure in the knowledge that somebody's got to beat the odds -- and if you think in a SuperOptimistic way, they're very likely to favor you.

Your new hat?

SECRET #67

Refer to pain as "sensation".

Adult preoccupation in post-modern society is now centered on constructing a personal security blanket. In the USA, this safe, comfortable way of living is referred to as "the good life" or "the American Dream."

The problem is that when you live 99% of your life in a dream, you are ill-prepared to deal with the real "speed bumps" of existence: realities like fire, death, dismemberment, blindness, terrorism, taxes, disease, hunger, pain, cruelty, bad drivers, and computer technology that goes on the fritz. Not to mention the lesser shocks of unexpected teenage pregnancy, rude waiters, blocked drains, and lost car keys.

The good news is, *pain does not need to be perceived as negative.* Every painful event can be a doorway to something that we can find valuable, truthful, insightful, and unique. So the next time something painful happens, tell yourself it's just part of the marvelous sensation of being alive. Here are a few mantras to get you started: "I will cherish and enjoy my pulled hamstring." "I will revel in my failed relationship." "I will make friends with my borderline personality disorder." By embracing the pain, you may find it lessens or disappears altogether.

SECRET #37

Remove shoes whenever possible.

The soul. The sole. This is not a coincidence. Almost every major internal organ can be affected by placing direct pressure on certain areas of the feet. Yet we encase our tootsies in leather or nylon, and let them fester in a dark, sweaty place for most of the day.

One of the best natural massages you can give your long-suffering feet is to walk barefoot through grass. Here you'll find a nonaddictive mood stabilizer called "herbacinium." Since each foot has thousands of itty-bitty fibrous nerve endings, soaking the herbacinium through your balls, heals, and toes and into the bloodstream can lower your heart rate by up to 14%. So the relaxation isn't just psychological, it's also physical.

In addition, by taking off your shoes, your feet can breath. And if they're breathing, chances are, so are you.

SECRET #92

Seek bad endings.

Lots of people think: "Oh, I screwed up." Or "Gosh, that was the wrong thing to do." Or "Gee, why on earth did I marry this bum?" But the SuperOptimist knows that any decision you make is a good decision for you -- even the "bad" ones. All decisions lead you to increased self-knowledge, and tragic decisions can lead you there faster if you are willing to learn from them. Every bad ending is a good beginning to something else, as well as a reminder to "never try that again." This secret has some powerful mojo to it. Give it a try!

NOTE: *The Wright brothers crashed more aircraft than they flew by a ratio of 27:1.*

SECRET #29

Make it a lungo.*

Many artists, writers, and inventors come up with their best ideas in the morning. Why? Because that's when the caffeine takes hold.

SuperOptimist findings suggest that moderate consumption (4-5 cups per day) of caffeine is not only preferable to a macchiato-free diet, it's mandatory if you expect to stay upbeat through the daily perturbations of human existence. You'll benefit from improved cognitive performance, alertness, and concentration. Moreover, caffeine is an ergogenic aid -- a substance that improves exercise capacity. And since the International Olympic Committee (IOC) removed caffeine from its list of banned substances in 2004, you can feel free to push the performance barrier.

How many cups of coffee are "too much"? Nobody knows for sure. Your body is your laboratory; be a self-diagnostician after your next heavy intake and take it from there.

lungo: long pull of espresso, preferably with 150mg+ of caffeine

SECRET #70

Give yourself an "A".

A, B, C, D, F -- Letter grades began in the 1800s for parents unable to grasp the concept of percentages on report cards. This practice of "grading" has become so commonplace that you're now graded on everything from kindergarten to corporate reviews to sexual performance. Want to make the system work for you? Think of anything you have done recently -- made a sandwich, taken a shower, walked the dog, etc. Now assign yourself a grade on the activity. Give yourself an "A." If you think you did a great job, give yourself an "A+." If you did a terrible job on it -- lost the dog, flooded the bathroom, cut part of your index finger off, give yourself a grade of "A-" for the task. No matter what you do, it's an "A." This way, even your worst work is still top quality.

Example:
JIM: "I forgot to put gas in my car, stopped dead on the highway and was late to work."
SUPEROPTIMIST: "Fantastic! You probably avoided a car accident from speeding. And you missed the time-wasting morning meeting. By cutting your work day in half, you were effectively twice as productive for the rest of the day! You get an A+!"
JIM: "I hadn't thought about it that way. Thanks!"

SECRET #9

Stop doubting yourself ; start doubting everyone else.

From a very early age -- for example, immediately upon leaving the birth canal -- a human being is programmed by parents, teachers, journalists, bosses, politicians, and religious leaders to think in pre-determined patterns. Most are focused on a tidy world of comparison, whether it be to Jesus, Madame Curie, Jackie Robinson, or a future member of Mensa who just scored 1580 on the SATs. In all cases, the bar is raised so high, it's practically impossible for anyone to clear.

Why are the authority figures of the world so insistent that we jump at their command? Because they've failed to clear the hurdle themselves! Thus, they need to shift some of their failure onto you. Remember that "the rules" are set by flawed humans. SuperOptimists are encouraged to question all those eager to impose their rigid set of limitations, principles, laws, tenets, requirements, speed limits, and HR advisories.

A program of SuperOptimist "active doubting" can lead you to a Tibetan shrine, Biosphere II, Florida nudist colony, congressional subcommittee, or a stripped down VW Beetle parked along the coast of Oahu. No matter where you end up, you'll be in the driver's seat.

SECRET #18

Festina Lente!

Five hundred years ago, hard-working Venetian Aldo Manuzio -- publisher of over 300 texts -- uttered the only two words for which we remember him today: "Festina Lente."*

His paradoxical advice of "slowing down to go faster" is a good guideline for whatever you work to build. The "haste" you need is not fast initial growth.   It's better to check and double-check the foundations before you work on the 97th floor -- or before you gather a crowd on the roof to admire the view.

Begin gradually, without too much investment, so you can learn from your mistakes while the risks are manageable.   Slowly add resources and train people while you learn and grow.

The SuperOptimist knows it's always a good time to slow down or even *stop working*.   You'll be 10 to 15 times as productive when you return to the task.

Translation: "hurry slowly"

SECRET #97

Develop an invisible friend.

That way, you'll always have moral support, someone to talk to, and never be alone. If someone thinks you are crazy -- talking to yourself -- all the better. Nobody bothers crazy people. And sometimes they get *free food.*

"Larry"

SECRET #48

Chance of victory: 100%.

The SuperOptimist knows -- at the start of any endeavor -- to assume that they'll win. History provides us with countless examples of conflicts that looked hopeless, and yet the "underdog" ultimately prevailed. One of the best compilations of such victories is the Holy Bible, or "Good Book." Taken only for its sports metaphors, this historical treatise is full of underdog tales: David versus Goliath, Moses versus Ramses, Jesus versus the high priests in Jerusalem, Judas vs. himself.

They all recount a simple SuperOptimist secret: The first step to winning the day is to believe you can win the day. And why not? It does not cost you any more money to assume you'll win, nor any extra work, nor staff, nor resources. No matter what's at stake, if you believe you'll come out the winner, you are 10 - 100 - 1000! times more likely to be that winner when the sun sets.

NOTE: *Muhammad Ali believed nobody could beat him, and he was only wrong 5 times in 21 years.*

19

SECRET #79

Half empty? Half full? Not your concern.

While philosophers can spend an eternity wondering whether a glass of water is half empty or half full, the SuperOptimist sees it for what it is -- a partially filled glass waiting to be sipped. 7 1/2 glasses more, and he will be well-hydrated for the day. 4 more after that, and he's super-hydrated!

The philosophy behind the SuperOptimist glass view? *If you don't need to worry about it -- then don't!* Let a committee of experts, professors, and doctoral candidates try to answer the unanswerable. Even the best minds can get stumped on the toughest problems, like these:

1. Why are there no words that rhyme with "orange"?
2. What color are things in the dark?
3. If Earth were struck by a giant meteor, who would survive and what would happen to real estate prices?

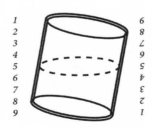

SECRET #95

At random moments, shout:
"Wait a minute. What's going on here?"

This simple act –– a seven word outburst -- serves to bring you (and anyone else who happens to be within earshot) into the *absolute present*.

No longer are you stuck in your own messy thought process, projecting some bleak misfortune that may happen to you in the future, or wallowing in some past mistake that everyone else has long since forgotten. Instead, you snap to full attention, the sound waking up you and everyone else to what's really going on! Additional benefits include frightening away potential muggers and making co-workers think you can see through their transparent facades.

In fact, your shout-out is one of the best examples of the Heisenberg Uncertainty Principle* in action: The observer not only changes events by his mere presence, but his presence also frequently surpasses the event in terms of importance. So go ahead. Shout and surpass the moment!

Werner Heisenberg, physicist, 1901-1976.

SECRET #24

Lose your first million.

Most people don't realize how easy it can be to make a million dollars. Yet if it weren't easy, 1 out of 110 Americans wouldn't be millionaires. Odds are in your favor once you realize how easy it is to be that "one."

The SuperOptimist must learn to risk big. Take a gamble and buy an apartment building on credit. Let go of fear and see what happens. Maybe you triple your money! Maybe you lose it all! There are countless stories of businessmen, inventors, artists, and above-ground pool manufacturers who made a small fortune, lost it all, and then *went on to make an even bigger fortune.*

That's because these successful entrepreneurs learned that money was never real in the first place. Especially when compared to a rock, an azalea, or a blueberry pie. The incredible good luck of losing a million dollars freed their thinking to understand that money was not security, it was not even a "tool." The true secret is that money is merely an idea, and the minute you imagine money, big money -- well, even $1,000,000.00 starts to seem like no big whoop.

SECRET #14

Own and wear a sarong.

Three million years ago, we were wild apes roaming the planet, with no need for constrictive clothing, underpants, or caps. Then came evolution, which led to less body hair (a plus) but the need for slacks and parkas (a minus). One way to recapture the freedom of our gorilla days is to forgo our usual attire and dress in a sarong.

A sarong is a large sheet of fabric, often wrapped around the waist and worn in a skirt-like fashion by men and women in southeast Asia and the Pacific islands, most particularly Indonesia and Malaysia. The fabric of a traditional sarong is brightly colored or printed with intricate patterns, often depicting animals, plants, rasta or rock 'n roll motifs, checkered or geometric patterns.

In America, men may initially feel nervous about the sarong and have the misguided idea that it's a "skirt for girls." Men should consider how comfortable it is to walk around only in a bath-towel -- or as it's called in Hawaii, "freeballin."

NOTE: Anytime you wear a sarong, it's a step closer to being on vacation, a favorite SuperOptimist pursuit.

23

SECRET #32

The past is not a nice neighborhood.

Guilt can be described as "the emotional luggage from the past making repeated trips around the baggage carousel of your mind." Take a quick look in the rear view mirror and there it is: the stock you could have bought for $1.25 that's worth $2.4 million today, the person you didn't marry who became a cable television star and is featured in revealing outfits in the pages of *InTouch* magazine, the family function you didn't attend where you could have patched things up with your grandfather, now deceased. By focusing on your errors, slights, gaffs, and screw-ups, you fail to remember even one of your very many (really too many to list here) good and kind acts. So don't let this past history/autopsy start, because it will end up dragging you down from your SuperOptimistic toehold in today. And today is all that matters!

SECRET #13

Act like a mallard.

If the anas platyrhynchos (duck) could not dismiss water from his back as easily as a shake of the tail, he would wind up 80 lbs of soggy feathers sunk to the bottom of Old Barnes Pond. Maintaining flotation is essential to his, and our, optimism. So seek out your local ducks. See how they do it. They don't absorb the water, therefore they don't get weighed down. Now you try it. Let that big deadline, or relationship issue, or chronic worry about your 401K, roll right off your spinal column. Give that problem an extra back kick with your heel as it nears your ankle for good measure. Boy, there's a lot to learn from ducks.

NOTE: *Paddling furiously in circles while looking completely calm is another good duck move worth study.*

SECRET #57

The most vitally important person on the planet right now? It's you.

At any given moment, the entire fabric of reality could be perched on your fitful consciousness and the world is only manifest because of you. Since you can't be certain which moment it is, you are best served by acting as if every moment is that moment of great importance!

Example:
You're shopping at Costco and bang your cart into a terrorist saboteur disguised as a chubby suburban housewife. You give him a look as if it was *his fault* you were crowding the aisle. This frightens him into thinking Federal Agents are keeping tabs on his every move and he abandons his plan to blow the place sky-high. You have just saved the world from a terrorist attack by shopping at Costco. You may never know you thwarted a nefarious plot -- but when you believe your existence is vital to the planet, even small actions become extra special acts of valor in the bigger scheme of things.

SECRET #45

Set no goals. Then marvel as you exceed them.

How many times do human beings set themselves up to fail? One universal example is the classic "New Year's Resolution." "I'm going to quit smoking." "I'm going to lose 25 pounds." "I'm going to write a best-selling suspense novel, sell it for $300,000, pay off my credit card debt, move the family to a warmer climate, and really start living!"

Setting unrealistic goals is a sure way to drive yourself into depression. Rather than look realistically at the situation, we crank ourselves up for a major achievement, step in a pothole right out of the gate, and go back to the "I'm a loser who's never going to get out of Fayetteville!" whine. Three packs a day and an extra slice of bundt cake follow shortly thereafter.

The SuperOptimist view? Maybe quitting smoking is a noble goal, but if it will cause you to kill your spouse, you should put it on the backburner. Maybe that quart of vanilla fudge nut swirl is what makes a night of insomnia tolerable. Maybe anonymous phone sex works. See where we're going here?

SECRET #45 - CONTINUED

Rather than set yourself up for complete and utter failure, how about turning the tables on that reluctant inner mountain climber with the rusted set of crampons? Today, set yourself up for major SuperOptimism -- by not setting any goals at all! Suddenly, anything you do will seem like an accomplishment. Getting out of bed! Putting the tea kettle on! Picking up the phone when it rings!

Who knows, without the pressure of a self-imposed Pike's Peak, you just might start writing that novel and forget about the long naps and bundt cake for awhile. You never know until you start lowering the bar!

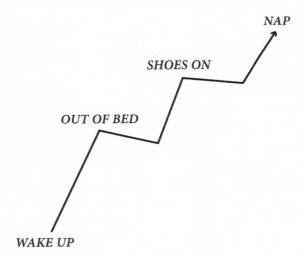

Chart 2: A good day's work.

SECRET #31

Caring may be hazardous to your health.

It is nice to take a strong interest in a person, a job, or a cause. But it's not necessarily an effective way to get anything accomplished! Physically, caring too much tightens the muscles and leads to stress. Mentally, over-caring releases too much adrenaline, flooding your body, jumbling thoughts and overstimulating the nervous system. In other words, rather than assisting you in peak functioning, caring can actually pull you down. So the next time you're in a situation in which the stakes are high, just say: "I don't care." This can quickly flip things in your favor, like a proper judo move.

BOSS: "I have bad news for you, you're fired."
EMPLOYEE: "I don't care."
BOSS: "What! You can't say that!"
EMPLOYEE: "I don't care."
BOSS: "Wha...Is this a trick?"
EMPLOYEE: "Yes."

NOTE: Joe Montana, possibly the greatest quarterback in the history of professional football, employed a spiritual advisor to help him empty his mind of all cares before a big game. Sound counter-intuitive? Not when you consider he sports 4 Super Bowl championship rings.

SECRET #6

You're a genius
(you just don't know it yet).

Do you experience any of the following: restlessness, irritability, grandiosity, overreaction, emotional intensity, diversity of thought, and rapidity of associational processes? Well, these are all highly characteristic of creative geniuses!

Geniuses tend to be individuals who aren't like other people. Take a guy like Casey Stengel.* Stengel said a lot of things that people didn't understand at first. Geniuses are like that. You can't expect them to act like a normal person. So if you're *not* acting "normal" right now, you're probably a genius. Congratulations!

baseball manager, 1890-1975

Quote: "Most ball games are lost, not won."

SECRET #51

Don't simply compliment another person.
Tell them they're the "world's best."

To be a true SuperOptimist means being of service to others. And a simple way of doing this is to offer everyone you happen upon a big helping of positive feedback. Most people depend on the judgment of others for their self-worth. So don't hold back. Give them what they long for -- your hearty assessment of how well they're doing.

You'd be amazed at how offering rich and meaty compliments can make a person feel so effervescent, they can't help but reflect this sudden rush of self-esteem back to you. Which makes it a win-win situation. Try it with friends, colleagues, the lady who passes your coffee out the window of the Dunkin' Donuts drive-thru. "Hey, Dunkin' Donuts gal! You're the world's best!"

NOTE: Sometimes you get free doughnut holes thanks to Secret #51.

SECRET #39

SuperOptimism 1, Satan 0.

Now for some really good news: there is no Devil. Or Hell. Or Purgatory. How can we be certain? Think about who invented this stuff. Human beings, that's who! The same flesh and blood, mistake-prone, imperfect knuckleheads who drop ketchup bottles on the floor of the supermarket ("Clean up in aisle 9!"), who drive their cars into each other on a daily basis, and who make predictions of Armageddon every year to scare people into line.

Even the big kahuna, Jesus, was human. "Christ also shared in their humanity" (Hebrews 2:14). So if you're wondering whether what you are about to do is a sin, "bad," evil, or that you're going "burn in Hell" for enjoying the simple pleasures of the world, forget it. Live, you imperfect creature, while you can! The SuperOptimist says it's all fine and dandy. Just don't kill anybody. And please, clean up after your dog. That's just common decency.

SECRET #2

Live beneath your means.

SuperOptimist Financial Tip: there's nothing more satisfying than not having your spirit crushed under the weight of a jumbo mortgage or a 19.7% APR. By the same token, driving a leased Mercedes makes little sense when a used Corolla will do. The money you save by not keeping up with the Joneses will accumulate faster than you can say "No-load mutual fund." Invest conservatively and you can be the first on your block to say "sayonara" to office drudgery and pursue your true calling. So don't be swayed by the notion of an "ownership society." All that means is more responsibility, taxes, insurance, and paperwork. The most precious commodities are available for free: air, sunshine, green grass, and your untethered imagination. Enjoy!

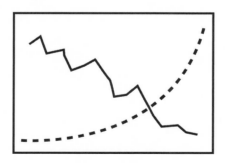

Wealth vs. Joy : where are you on the continuum?

SECRET #20

Put the concept of "work" into perspective.

Before the industrial revolution (a mere hundred years ago), the average workday was only 3 hours long. Then machines were introduced, along with the first advertisements. A period of rapid progress was immediately followed by the Great Depression. Suddenly, being "fully employed" made you the envy of your neighbors, and working at least 8 hours a day defined a modern citizen as a "success."

Since then, putting work at the center of modern life has led to 7-day work weeks, accompanied by clinical depression, absentee parenting, and rampant consumerism. Additionally, in periods of rising employment, statistics show a rise in industrial accidents, alcohol abuse, and illness in direct proportion to the good economic climate. They don't call it a "job" for nothing.

Fortunately, the SuperOptimist knows he is more than the sum total of his paycheck or the title on his business card. In fact, rather than work 50 weeks a year for 2 weeks of freedom, he attempts to invert the formula and work *2 weeks a year for 50 weeks of freedom.* This may mean a sacrifice of worldly possessions, to which he replies, "Who needs more than two shoes?" Invert the 52 - 2 formula and see how good it feels.

SECRET #3

Enjoy the side effects.

In any experience, the truly unexpected is the most exciting element you can look for. The odd smell that cannot be placed. The "detour" sign at your exit on the highway. The dizziness that accompanies an over-the-counter allergy medication. If there were no interesting side effects, the world would be too predictable, and no one would hit their head getting in or out of an automobile.

Metal helmets, once popular, have been replaced by the modern baseball cap due to the many unpleasant side effects of wearing a helmet to work. Is this progress?

SECRET #54

Dipsy. Dodo. Discharge.

A SuperOptimist is always exercising facial muscles in an upward slant for two reasons. One is that he feels in fine fettle a vast majority of the time, which puts a smile on his face. The second is that he knows how beneficial laughter is to maintaining an elevated mood in himself, as well as those around him. In fact, a SuperOptimist is a "student of laughter" and subscribes to the following suppositions about why we react with a hearty guffaw to certain situations:

1: *reverse dipsy-doodle supposition*. It's amusing when the opposite of what we expect to happen, happens. For example, when our boss falls out of his chair.

2: *smarter than that dodo supposition*. When we chortle at another person's bum luck or mistake. For example, when our boss falls out of his chair.

3: *liberation discharge supposition*. Humor lets us release the pent up emotions inherent in a stressful situation. For example, when our boss falls out of his chair.

Put these theories into your SuperOptimist Utility Belt. They can never be overused. And don't forget, laughter is also good for the abdominal muscles.

SECRET #5

Wait not -- want not.

One of the main causes of stress? Waiting. Waiting for a bus, waiting on a ticket line, waiting for a table at a restaurant, waiting for a customer service representative to pick up the phone. Minimizing this frustrating "down time" is a key to maintaining a SuperOptimistic outlook.

Question the group dynamic. The movie that just made $120 million in its opening weekend, is it really any good? What about the Japanese/Moroccan fusion restaurant with the line out the door? Often going against the flow of the crowd will score you better seats to the opera, a friend that will keep you interested in a conversation, or a business opportunity that everyone's overlooked. The SuperOptimist knows that a personal choice always trumps the popular one!

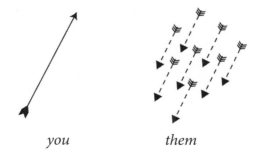

you   *them*

SECRET #3

Put your feet near water.

In ancient times, man's connection with the planet's hydrosphere (aka "water") was more intimate and immediate. We had rain gods with exciting names like Tlaloc, Hoya, Tonenlili, and Eurus. We crossed rivers by wading, rather than by toll bridge.

Placing your feet in close proximity to "aqua pura" lets you connect with lunar tidal rhythms, ancient Earth powers, and forces you up from the couch. What kind of water should you seek out? Among the SuperOptimist recommendations are the following: trout streams, tropical beaches, hot tubs, boat docks, wading pools, reflecting ponds, white-water rapids, waterfalls, geysers, canals, inland waterways, bubbling mineral springs, and winding creeks. In a pinch, an open fire hydrant will do.

SECRET #28

Love your worst problem best.

That's right. Love it. Embrace it. Cherish it. If it's a good solid problem, you are incredibly lucky to have the issue to grapple with. Alcoholism, diabetes, dwarfism, eczema, eating disorders, authority issues, head lice, ADD, OCD, DMZ, clubbed feet. Chances are you'll wrestle with your problem for years. Maybe you get over it. Maybe you find a solution. Maybe you don't.

How can a problem be lovable? Because of what it can give back to you. Things like patience. Things like perspective. Things like understanding of nature at the deepest levels.

QUOTABLE: *"It's not that I'm so smart, it's just that I stay with the problems longer."* - Albert Einstein

SECRET #108

Never be photographed while eating.

Nobody looks good when sticking a forkful of hot Chicken Marsala in their pie-hole. If the photograph appears in the wrong publication, it's a sure-fire career killer. In England, it's actually illegal to show the queen eating. Should you see cameras where you happen to be dining, request a private room. You'll be glad you did.

The international "Stop! No photos por favor!" hand sign. Know when to use it and when it's not enough.

SECRET #60

When in doubt, let loose with a sports cheer. e.g. "Go Birds!"

Should you find yourself at a loss for words in a tense situation -- say, a speech in front of eleven thousand colleagues, giving a toast at your best friend's wedding, or that special moment with a new love when you're expected to declare your intimacy in a verbal manner -- a good ol' shout out to your favorite team will break the ice and be universally understood. And while everyone starts talking sports, you can figure out your next move. Super Bowl? No, SuperOptimism!

NOTE: *Give yourself extra credit for throwing something when emitting your heartfelt cheer.*

SECRET #18

Straight is great.

There are three main reasons why people slump. 1) the general force of gravity which tends to pull us down and collapse our spinal column. 2) the tendency to lean forward and direct our attention when we work with tools. 3) being coerced into some exhausting and mind-numbing task like operating a sheet-metal screw-press or working a factory assembly line.

SuperOptimists stand up straight, and when they walk ahead, they thrust the chest forward, heart open to all potential experiences and opportunities. This not only sends a message of power and confidence to all those who see you coming towards them. But inside, your erect posture helps improve circulation, centers your chi (energy), and, combined with deep breathing, improves oxygenation of the blood. This gives you a feeling of relaxation, while helping your body fight disease. All this, from going straight! Posture, that is!

NOTE: *You can test your posture right now by simply balancing this book on your head. This is also a great way to develop poise for future modeling assignments!*

SECRET #14

TV off? SuperOptimism on!

Television is the Great American Discontent Machine, and the average person watches it 3 1/2 hours a day. That's 25 hours a week of subjecting yourself to riches you don't have, body types that only exist on a surgeon's table, and advertising that promises you a better life, based on your choice of soda pop, lawn care product, and power-train warranty. Is it any wonder that clinical depression is on the rise?

Take the story of Bhutan, a small, idyllic Buddhist kingdom situated between India and China, where TV was banned from all households. Peace and joy were in great abundance. In the words of Bhutan's King Singye Wangchuck, "gross national happiness is more important than gross national product."

But then the king lifted his ban on television and the Internet. Suddenly, a posse of cable operators converged on the tiny kingdom and offered multiple channels of professional sports, ultra-violence, sexual betrayal, and home shopping networks The result? Bhutan has begun its slide into the realm of the ordinary, and even long-time monks are finding themselves spacing out in front of "The Real Gilligan's Island."

43

SECRET #14 - CONTINUED

Whatever the "programming," TV is proven to negatively impact our sense of well-being. In fact, it's been estimated that one extra hour of TV a week causes you to spend an extra $4.00. That's a hundred bucks more a week for the average viewer!

The SuperOptimist does not have a cable hookup or a satellite dish. Instead, he or she turns to his or her own imagination, and creates stories which make Disney and Time Warner look like small fry. Practice turning your inner mind into an IMAX® screen, and you can go anywhere. Without commercial interruption!

SECRET #44

You're h-a-p-p-y.

You just *forgot* that you are happy. Wait! How could it happen? How could you forget something as basic as this?

It's easy in our intense, modern, multichannel, multi-tasking environment to become so distracted that you forget you are basically fine and dandy. So if you're trying to save time by doing three or five things at once -- stop now! A growing body of scientific research shows that this kind of behavior can take longer than doing things one at a time, and may leave you with reduced brainpower to perform each task.

The SuperOptimist knows that happiness is actually the natural state of humanity -- before you pile on the impossible deadlines, self-inflicted stress, and superfluous goals that lead decent folk to lose their noodles. Happy is always inside you. It just may require a lot of unplugging and unpiling to find it.

NOTE: Chronic high-stress multitasking is linked to short-term memory loss. If you can't remember the last 3 secrets you read in this book, you're already showing symptoms!

SECRET #61

Let history decide.

"The definition of genius is that it acts unconsciously; those who have produced immortal works, have done so without knowing how."

- William Hazlitt, English essayist and SuperOptimist

Why worry about whether the work you are doing is any "good"? Every artist, musician, emperor, pharaoh, and king who has said "this is my masterpiece" was wrong, and it was only with 100 (or 500) years of perspective that humanity could judge what was the "good stuff" and what was overwrought ego posturing or self-aggrandizing jack-offery.

Just think how many authors have been blocked by the fear that if they were not writing the "great American novel" for their generation, they may as well give up entirely and be a barrista at Starbucks. Multiply the number of Starbucks by 4 and that's the number of writers who stopped at page 1. Rather than judge your own work, direct 110% of your energy into doing it. Put the pedal to the metal, and let history decide.

SECRET #77

And the universe will thank you.

Even if you don't regularly donate to the United Way, AmeriCares, or the ACLU, it's great to have a favorite charity in mind, because the next time someone asks you for a donation, you can say: "I donate to the _____ _____."

NOTE: *If you are stuck for a charity, allow us to suggest Bat Conservation International (www.batcon.org). These wise nocturnal folk have been studying and preserving amazing mammals for over 20 years. SEE: Secret #81.*

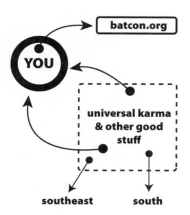

SECRET #93

Talk to strangers. Then listen.

Society prefers us to "fear strangers." This helps justify expensive color-coded security defense systems, border patrols between countries, and multi-billion-dollar budgets for the F-22 stealth jet fighter.

But SuperOptimists understand that fear is an overused emotion. It's so bad for you to walk around in a constant state of agitation; it's imperative to find a way to *devalue fear.*

One of the best ways to put fear in its place is to talk to strangers. Strangers represent the unknown, a world outside our own bodies. But since most of the universe is outside our own bodies, it can only help us to get comfortable with "that stuff outside," rather than fearing what's there. Take the first easy step. Talk to a stranger. See what happens. It's 7 to 10 times more likely you'll learn a vital truth than be assaulted with expletives.

NOTE: *Talking to strangers while in a movie line is how comedian Chevy Chase met producer Lorne Michaels, was subsequently cast on "Saturday Night Live", became a celebrity, and went on to a life of intermittent glamor and back pain in Hollywood.*

SECRET #19

Even if you don't believe in God, She believes in you.

Agnostic? Atheist? Devil-worshipper? Muslim? Protestant? Wiccan? *God doesn't care.* She just wants you to be happy in whatever you do. So long as you respect the choices of others, and don't force your will on any defenseless man, woman, child, dog, snail, starfish, or smaller being. God's not a micromanager. God is your cornerwoman in the great boxing match of life.

SuperOptimist Epistle 1:4: You are a child of God no matter what type of odd personal behavior you're into. So just be the best possible version of you, and don't waste your time judging others or worrying about how they might be judging you. God bless.

SECRET #26

Embrace the nuts in your life.

Anytime you pop open a can of mixed nuts, you're doing yourself a favor. Nuts were unfairly labeled as a "high fat" food when America was told that eating fat makes you fat. The truth: Nuts are a natural, renewable, "green," vegan, organic food; in other words, they are perfect for your body.

Some 30 years ago, 30,000 Seventh Day Adventists agreed to participate in a study of their dietary habits. Those eating nuts daily had a 59% lower risk of fatal coronary heart disease. If mixed nuts work for these nuts, surely they'll work for you!

SECRET #15

Go to your room.

For the Buddha to arrive at total enlightenment, he needed to part company with his family and friends and wander in solitude for six years. If that seems excessive, we suggest creating a haven to which you can escape on a regular basis, and place into perspective whatever you currently have on your plate. This can be as elaborate as a house in the country, or as simple as a door with a double lock. It's a place where the phone won't ring, the significant other won't knock, and your neighbors won't know where to find you. Are you there right now? Good. Stay there. Sooner or later something great will happen.

SECRET #10

Look, up in the sky!

Big, isn't it? And always changing. Filled with possibilities, from sunrise to sunset. Nighttime especially. Why, until recently, humans used to study the sky with the fascination they now devote to a new 43-inch plasma screen HDTV ("Look at that sharpness and depth, it could almost be real."). The sky was the original reality show, and the SuperOptimist knows that looking at the sky has immediate positive benefits including:

- reconnection to nature
- advance info on what to wear
- constant reminder of change
- beautiful color palette for re-use
- good eye exercise
- improves posture
- provides signs & omens
- looks like a big lava lamp

Note: Looking at the sky in 1514 gave Copernicus the idea that the sun was at the center of the solar system. This new idea gave rise to advances such as calculus, rationality, and Levelor® blinds.

SECRET #107

Skip therapy today.

The word "shrink" is a downer. Nobody in life wants to shrink. We want to grow! Yet due to malfunctions in upbringing, many of us are neurotics to some degree. Does that mean we should sign ourselves over to the nearest psychoanalyst and rub his couch raw with our "issues"?

A SuperOptimist subscribes to the notion that *our weaknesses are also our strengths.* Therefore, if you're too sensitive in social situations, you don't have to spend a lifetime with a therapist to overcome your "shyness." Accept this flaw and *move forward.* Use your extreme sensitivity to write, paint, or theorize in relative solitude. Conversly, if you have anger management issues, channel them into pursuits such as kickboxing, demolition derbies, or covert police activity.

For the few folks truly "out to lunch," there are drug treatments that may help you get better; altering your brain chemistry can lead to miraculous upswings. At least it's superior to moaning on a couch for the next 20 years wringing your hands over how you got dealt a bum DNA strand by "bad mommy." Accept your weakness, damage, and broken parts as a strength, and who knows how far you can go.

SECRET #42

Hug your hypothalamus.

Fact: the more direct sunlight you absorb through the eyes, the more SuperOptimistic your outlook upon life! Here's the science behind the salvation: UV rays shoot into the eye, enter the retina and filter through to the pineal gland. This produces melatonin, a chemical that gives a boost to the hypothalamus gland. The hypothalamus controls a whole range of vital functions, including mood, sex drive, and metabolism. Sunlight is also an indirect provider of Vitamin D and may prevent some cancers.

The importance of sunlight on cellular functioning cannot be emphasized enough. And fortunately for the residents of Alaska, North Dakota, and Minnesota, the brain can be goosed to believe that it's receiving sunlight, even when the body is stuck indoors. A UV light source emitting 130 watts of sun substitute will suffice.

SECRET #11

Focus on the previous small thing.

Everyone's always on the alert for "the next big thing." Yet a key to staying sane and at peace is to notice and appreciate the little idea. Don't ignore the fork at the table when you sit down to eat; pick it up and admire the ingenuity it took to craft such a simple, yet perfect, tool. The same goes for salt and pepper shakers, the butter dish, and the napkin ring. Once you begin treasuring under-appreciated objects like these, it's only a matter of time before you think of some simple, yet vital, invention that could be as popular as the fork or salt shaker. Perhaps a combination fork and salt shaker, all in one! The salt-fork? The forshaken? The salforker!

What extremely valuable new product can be made from these common parts?

SECRET #36

Make today a complete experiment!

Il celeberrimo esperimento dell'argento vivo fu realizzato da Torricelli nella primavera del 1644 a Firenze. Torricelli riemp" di mercurio un tubo di vetro aperto ad una delle estremit^. Poi, tenendo serrata con un dito l'estremit^ aperta, rovesci˜ il tubo in una bacinella contenente mercurio. Osserv˜ allora che la colonna di mercurio scendeva solo parzialmente, fermandosi ad un'altezza di circa 76 cm.

SECRET #68

Assume the position!

Kurt Vonnegut said if he had one regret in life, it would be that he didn't stretch more. He wasn't speaking about his imagination, but about his torso. Testing our physical elasticity not only helps us get the kinks out, but aids the blood flow to all our extremities, and ultimately releases dopamine within our brain -- the key chemical to a SuperOptimistic life! The poses the SuperOptimist favors are derived from the Chinese kung fu internal arts of Tai Ji and Bagua Zhang.

NOTE: *To enter one of the SuperOptimist poses, simply move your body around freely until you feel a sharp pain somewhere. The pain signals you are in one of the correct poses. Stay in the pose until the pain recedes, then seek a different pose using this same method. (minimum 45 minutes daily)*

SECRET #50

The less you want it, the faster you'll get it.

Why is it that the girl or boy of our dreams almost never materializes, yet we can always attract somebody who we're not the slightest bit interested in? Why is it when we're in a real rush, there's never a parking spot, but when we've got all the time in the world, somebody pulls out right in front of us at the dry cleaners?

A lesson here? Remove the word "need" from your vocabulary. If you don't give a monkey's toss what happens at any given moment, the universe will expand in direct proportion to your disinterest.

EXERCISE: Act completely aloof at your next job interview. Chances are, they'll make you an offer. Refuse -- and they'll up it to a management position. Shake your head no, and boom! Senior vice presidency. Move towards the door waving goodbye, and they'll drop to their knees and plead with you to take a seat on the board. Walk out the door without agreeing to their terms and you'll be 5 times closer to your real goal!

SECRET #40

When the Lord is ready to speak to you, have a pen and paper handy.

Always carry a small notebook and a Uniball Vision Micro Pen® with you, just in case. By writing down your next good idea, invention, philosophic screed, or important phone number, you won't miss out on a potentially life-changing experience. SuperOptimists believe it's vitally important to put pen to paper (or chalkboard, canvas, Wacom tablet, rock), because that act is like ye olde hero dragging the magic fire out of the sky. In committing to paper, you convert the invisible and immaterial to 100% real in black and white.*

NOTE: "Black and white" is merely a figure of speech. Colors may be substituted at your discretion.

SECRET #25

Boredom is power.

"Boredom excites imagination." Or so wrote Fyodor Dostoevsky, author of "Crime and Punishment", and 3 other well-regarded works of literature. Despite his Russian propensity for gloom, Fyodor definitely exhibited SuperOptimist tendencies.

For the SuperOptimist realizes that the mind will always seek an escape route from the cage of boredom eventually. Even if the route is up over the craggy Himalayas, and each step is hard, hard, work, the mind will seek it nonetheless. Just think how good it will feel to climb up out of boredom and conquer that mountain. Take that first step now and we'll see you at the top!

This way out.

SECRET #22

Excessive speed can save lives.

In any new or daring task, it's not a bad idea to charge ahead as fast as possible. Leonardo da Vinci believed that it was vitally important for artists to work quickly to capture the "first flash of inspiration." Ralph Waldo Emerson concurred, saying, "In skating over thin ice, our safety is in our speed."

It is also the advice of the Japanese master swordsman Miyamoto Musashi, who described the "sekka no atari" -- or "lightning strike" -- as charging in with strong legs, strong body, and strong arms combined for maximum speed. As he plunged into battle, Musashi had no time for worry, fear, doubt, or regret. He relied on having mushin, or "empty mind," to detach from whether he'd emerge victorious or chopped in half. Foreseeing the possible outcomes could serve no practical purpose. The truth would be revealed through action. So stop foreseeing and just go, go, go!

NOTE: *This secret stands in complete opposition to statements elsewhere in this book; for instance, Secret #18. Further proving that contradiction is not feared, but embraced, by the true SuperOptimist who savors a complex universe.*

SECRET # 108

Compare yourself downward.

Did you know that Academy Award losers die 4 years earlier than Academy Award winners?* That's 1,460 days of life snuffed out due to a subjective judgment passed by others on a single performance.

The reason for this startling fact: The losers unconsciously spend the rest of their lives comparing upwards, instead of down. In the case of Oscar nominees who go home empty-handed, many of them harbor resentments against the winners until the day they (prematurely) die, along with hating the guts of the Academy of Motion Picture Arts and Sciences, their agents, their lawyers, the editors at Variety, and the entire Hollywood community. In their minds, they deserved that statue and now the odds are great that they may never get another shot at one as long as they live!

Sure, the losers may mouth the words "I'm just lucky to be here, in the company of these other fine actors," but how many believe it, live it, and are truly happy for the winner? In fact, unless they know how to process this loss SuperOptimistically, they're on the road to ill-health and bad fortune.

*Redelmeier and Singh, *Anals of Internal Medicine*, May 2001

Instead of obsessing over another person's success, look over your shoulder at a screw-up. How about that old roommate who was always borrowing your favorite sweater when you were both in college. You know, the one who developed the dependency on prescription drugs and is now living in the basement of his mother's house.

Start any comparison with those less fortunate than yourself, rather than those who have more*, and you'll be 3 steps closer to SuperOptimism.

*NOTE: "More" is a technical term used by the SuperOptimist to define the combined problems of money, power, fame, good looks, family status, height, skill, 4.0 GPA, influence, and premium real estate location. All of these are potential impediments to achieving SuperOptimism.

SECRET #49

Access your unlimited secret power.

"Your imagination, my dear fellow, is worth more than you imagine," said Louis Aragon, poet-novelist, surrealist, and SuperOptimist. If Aragon sounds too vague, consider Thomas Alva Edison's more nuts-and-bolts understanding: "To invent, you need a good imagination and a pile of junk." So no matter what your life situation is today -- even if it resembles a disorganized yard sale -- activating and celebrating your personal power of imagination is the SuperOptimist's first step to improving things. If you can just imagine a better situation, you're more than 1/2 way to actually being there.

What is it? Who invented it? Who needs it? All good questions to stimulate the imagination.

SECRET #62

Learn to levitate above the problem.

For years, the practice of levitation has been the sole province of mediums and magicians. With mediums, levitation is claimed as a result of contact with a dead person, and is for the most part unverifiable. With magicians, a series of invisible wires, wenches, and pulleys are used to give the illusion of a person able to float above the ground.

However, neither is appropriate for the SuperOptimist, since they both involve outward manifestations of the term "rise above." What we do instead is *levitate on the inside,* to mentally climb above the issue that is festering within us.

Step 1. Identify the problem. This can be anything; for example, the chicken from the freezer is not defrosting as quickly as desired.

Step 2. Visualize the problem, then imagine you are rising above it like a cloud rising over a mountain. Physically place the frozen chicken on the floor. It will look small and inconsequential down there as it defrosts.

NOTE: *This example does not work in homes with dogs.*

SECRET #89

Even Elle Macpherson isn't "Elle Macpherson".*

Rather than feeling substandard to genetic miracles, remember that the "beautiful people" may not be exactly what they seem. As humans, they're still liable to run their car off the road (Oscar nominee James Dean), suffer from debilitating clinical depression (Pulitzer Prize-winning author William Styron), or channel their artistic talents into very poor choices (amateur painter Adolf Hitler). So why waste time comparing yourself to these famous creatures, all of whom have had problems and issues and body odor?

SuperOptimist contra-indictor: The more famous someone is, the less you want to be like them. Remember, at this very moment, an A-list celebrity is crying to her $250 an hour "life coach" about someone even prettier/smarter/better-connected than she is. Further research: Glance at a National Enquirer the next time you're at the supermarket -- and be glad you're not on the cover.

real name: Eleanor Gow

SECRET #55

Turn yourself into a fictional character.

Lots of folks create a fiction to justify their aberrant behavior. Take the "Three Bills" - Clinton, Cosby, and Gates. They're always receiving humanitarian awards, honorary degrees, and accolades. This is due to their enormous gift at telling stories about what great guys they are and how much they do for other people. Of course, at the end of the day, they've got two feet, two hands, and make gross errors of judgment just like you.

So remember, it's the story you start telling about who you are and what you are that sets your ship on a course of adventure through the high seas of life. Since it's *your* story, and you're making it up, you may as well make up a total whopper. Why say "I'm working this crap job bussing tables at Denny's" when you can say "I'm an undercover CIA operative on the lookout for potential trouble spots, starting with table 103!"

SECRET #30

Tip everybody.

You can't take it with you, so why not spread the wealth. Especially to those who least expect it. You might just get treated better! As an experiment, go into the office of your superior and give him $5. When he asks what it's for, you can say: "That's a tip for being such a good manager, enjoy!" It's worth the $5 to see your boss try to figure out what just happened.

The "wealth funnel." A SuperOptimist measures true wealth by exactly how much he is ready to give away at a moment's notice. This is calculated by a simple SuperOptimal math formula: (Give more) x (have less) = much better. Bonus: you'll end up with less clutter!

SECRET #8

Avoid the "future gap".

Despite being alive in this very moment, human beings have a tendency to want to "know" the future. Folks imagine a "career track" at work. At home they wonder about the "future of the relationship." The United States government encourages us to believe in "social security" and legally requires citizens to pay exorbitant taxes so they can invest in the invisible future of 2074 A.D.

The aspiring SuperOptimist can take a lesson from Nobel Prize-winning Danish physicist Niels Bohr. Professor Bohr conducted countless scientific experiments where he would try to guess the real outcome of events imagined beforehand. With the best theoretical models available, he still could not predict the future any better than a drunken tourist at a craps table in Las Vegas. Professor Bohr summed up his career of deep scientific thought by saying: "Prediction is very difficult, especially about the future."

Bohr proves that no matter how smart you are, you can't reliably predict 5 days from now, much less 50 years. That's why the SuperOptimist believes that the "good time" is not in some imagined far distant future, but in every tiny moment of existence at this very moment right now. And now. And now. And...now.

SECRET #70

The brain is your computer.
Reboot at any time.

Do you ever say to yourself, "I'm having a bad day! I was late for the train, my boss gave me the stink-eye. Nothing is going right, someone up there doesn't like me." Each successive bad thing brings on more self-defeating thoughts, until the "day is shot" and you're waiting for it to be over. Some people can turn a bad day into a week, a month, even convince themselves their life is a pre-ordained failure, just because they spill some coffee on their shirt or leave their cell phone at home.

Nonsense! For the SuperOptimist, a couple of bad moments in the course of 24 hours is nothing! Simply look at your brain as a computer which has become frozen, stuck, or infected with a "doubt & fear virus." Hit the RESTART button. Rebooting is as easy as closing your eyes, dumping the memory of what's just occurred, and reprogramming the self with the following language: "Reboot, Restart, Reframe, it's the best day of my wonderful life, starting...now!"

NOTE: *No license from Microsoft® required.*

SECRET #46

Know when to fold them.

Vacuuming the den. Painting a fence. Rehabbing a 1975 Schwinn 3-speed. It's the simple things in life that teach us the most. Here at the Academy for SuperOptimism, one of our favorite activities is the proper folding of a T-shirt. You will get great satisfaction from this simple exercise in hand-eye coordination. And when your T-shirts are crisp and wrinkle-free, there's a good chance you will be too! If you wear tee's that have been properly folded, you can expect your days to be filled with compliments. Among the examples: "Have you been working out?" "Have you lost weight?" "Are you having an affair?"

T-shirt provided to soldiers of Rome about the time of the Emperor Julius Caesar, 52 B.C. Don't we have it better now? (Add to your gratitude list.)

SECRET #21

Magnet vs. Mountain.

As every potential SuperOptimist adapting to a brave new feeling of positive energy discovers, there can be a few rough spots on the highway to total happiness. Newton's Third Law of Motion, with it's "equal and opposite reaction," explains it scientifically. But it can seem that just when life's getting good, a force of malign magnet voodoo sends some evil ju-ju your way.

The SuperOptimist welcomes the new problem as a sure sign of movement in a positive direction. So, while the natural inclination upon being hit with nasty magnet voodoo is to fight the negative force and try to resist the "bad news," the counter-intuitive trick is actually preferable: *don't fight the magnet.* Instead, relax into your perceived "failure." Look at it optimistically: "I've spent some time at the peak, having it good, now I am offered the tremendous opportunity to learn to enjoy myself in far worse conditions!"

The more you practice the acceptance of the cycle of bad magnet and good mountain, the more time you will spend in the clouds and less in the weeds. Remember, everyone can hit a rocky stretch, and slide back into old patterns of non-optimistic thought, but as you practice SuperOptimism on a daily basis you'll find that no matter what kind of bad mojo the magnet tries to stick to you, the mental discipline of SuperOptimism can elevate you to a feeling of being at the mountaintop, freshly swept by the rain, sun, wind, and fair skies.

NOTE: *Never face an adversary or problem head-on. A SuperOptimist avoids fighting force with more force; rather we try an "alternate route." (See Secret #99.)*

SECRET #34

While you may make mistakes, you yourself are not one!

Mistakes are human, and humans are fallible creatures. You are a human, therefore you are fallible and will make mistakes. Plenty of them. For the good of all concerned, a SuperOptimist never projects where his mistakes might lead. (Example: you leave your wallet on the train. Thoughts: "My entire identity has been stolen, my credit cards violated, and my sure-to-win lotto ticket's gone! I'm a complete bonehead for this idiot move!") Instead of such negative projection, the SuperOptimist recognizes that everyone makes mistakes. Enjoying and appreciating the miscue is the challenge. How one reacts and moves on shows whether you have absorbed the SuperOptimist mind-think! In this case, "Hurray, I get to buy a new wallet" is the appropriate response.

The five-leaf clover is a rare mutation of the common four-leaf clover. A genetic screw-up or extra-lucky charm? The answer is obvious to the SuperOptimist!

SECRET #9

Wool is your friend.

On a chilly day, there's nothing better to keep you comfy than a nice, natural, 100% wool hat. Or gloves. Or sweater. Besides the fact that being warm and snug helps you even in the midst of whatever challenges you may face, there's the added benefit -- wearing wool provides your friendly sheep with a day job. If not for the wearing of wool, sheep would be ignored -- or just lamb chop dinners -- neither of which is as positive as being a synergistic partner in an eco-friendly "green" garment industry. So let's take a lesson from the friendly sheep and seek comfortable synergies. The planet you save may be your own.

SECRET #81

On the contrary!

The SuperOptimist knows that information passed on to us as "fact" is often completely erroneous. Take the notion that bats are scary, neck-biting rats with wings and should be feared at all costs. Au contraire! Bats are gentle, wise, intelligent creatures. They pollinate plants and eat insects. A little brown bat may eat 600 mosquitoes in an hour. Bats don't poison the environment and are cheaper than bug lights. So if our opinion of bats has been hijacked, where else have we been misinformed?

If you've been told something is bad for you, this is a sure sign that it merits a closer look. And don't listen to us. Make up your own mind, it's one of the only freedoms left.

Man's other best friend?

SECRET #104

Question authority.
And everybody else too.

There's no shortage of people who'd like to tell you what to do with your life. Take self-help authors, for instance. Here's a group that outwardly preach the ability to fix problems and attain perfection in seven steps or less. However, when in their homes with the shades drawn, they are just as angry, foul-mouthed, and imperfect as you are. Perhaps more so. Scratching their backsides, yelling at their kids, sneaking glances at pornography, and greedy for even more residuals on their DVD sales. Just like everybody!

Remember, despite their confident, toothy grins, these "experts" are not their book jacket photos. What they (and you) can learn from SuperOptimism is to laugh at our ridiculous foibles, and re-think what makes them unhappy in the first place. Hint: Maybe the problem starts with calling something a "problem."

NOTE: *The only advice you should follow is your own personal truth. With just this secret alone, you are nine times more likely to find it!*

SECRET #74

All chairs are hard, not "easy".

The Marquis de Sade could not have invented a more exquisite means of torture than this simple device. Whether it be antique, ergonomic, or folding, the chair is a machine for keeping a human fixed in one place. If we didn't have them, people would be running about, naturally curious, exploring and interacting with the world. But because of the way modern industrial society works, humans are trained from childhood to sit in chairs for long periods, much the way puppies are taught to become so familiar with the leash that they are uncomfortable without their collar.

This is not to say you should never sit in a chair. After all, it is rather awkward to remain standing in a reception area when there's four-legged furniture available. But you should be wary. Know any rock stars who did it all slack-bottom in a chair? Generals? Artists? Anybody? We didn't think so.

NOTE: *The exception being the wheelchair-bound super-genius Stephen Hawking, a SuperOptimist who demonstrates the power of Secret #36.*

SECRET #76

Blame it on the Bossa Nova.

Ballet, hoe-down, break, watusi, jazz, tap, modern, pole -- the Surgeon General's report, "Physical Activity and Health", gives strong supporting evidence of the physiological benefits of dance on the cardiovascular and musculoskeletal systems, and on the functioning of metabolic, endocrine, and immune systems.

Recommendations from the ten major federal and nonfederal organizations that were partners in the report agree that weight-bearing exercise such as dancing should be performed daily for a minimum of thirty minutes at moderate intensity, increasing gradually in endurance for greater benefits. Start shaking it today; your pancreas will thank you tomorrow.

One of several internal organs that would like to be your dance partner.

SECRET #80

Grab a pencil and shout "Hallelujah"!

Whenever you feel tired, dyspeptic, or out-of-sorts, taking out a pen and paper and writing down all the positives you may be ignoring is a good way of refocusing your mind. Moving your arm in circular motions has been proven to counteract the negative voices, and remind you of all the wonderful blessings you have going for you right at this very moment.

Sample list:

I'm still above ground.
I can breathe through both nostrils.
I'm not Michael Jackson.
I'm in a room with baseboard heating.
My coffee is cold, but I still have some left.

SECRET #7

When you've had all you can take,
take another slice.

Are you in the midst of suffering the worst physical, emotional, or mental agony you've ever experienced? The natural impulse is to try to hop out of the burning hot frying pan as fast as you can. But the very movement of hopping around can burn your feet even more and land you in a worse spot.

The SuperOptimist version of handling even the most gruesome and ghastly of torments is to ask the universe for another supersized helping. Preparing yourself for *an even "worser" worst* -- when you think it's already as bad as it can be -- actually confuses the mind, and your suffering diminishes in proportion to your willingness to suffer more. Also, you build up a tolerance to pain, like a callus, so the longer you're in pain, the less you'll notice it. Ride any wave of horrid, stinky hellfire and you'll become more optimistic by a power of 4!

SECRET #38

The weather is always nice.

Sometimes when the weather seems "bad" -- rainy, snowy, awful, terrible -- it is a fine exercise for the SuperOptimist to run out the door and experience the truth of it. No umbrellas or gloves. No hat or jacket. Just run out there and get wet and if it feels good, scream and howl and let your body awaken to it. Feel the truth in your body, not what the 5-day forecast is telling you. You will almost immediately discover that the weather may not be bad at all -- but actually is quite stimulating.

Bonus points: Do it naked.

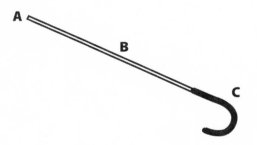

The SuperOptimist Umbrella:
A) good luck B) shaft C) rubber handle

SECRET #112

Create your own holidays.

Every holiday known to man has started as a positive exercise and then been co-opted by corporate interests, sucking all the real meaning and joy out of it. To think that Jesus rising from the dead is a cue for chocolate bunny rabbits is a case in point.

That said, there's no reason to follow the herd down to the mall every time some representative from Hallmark yells "March!" Step aside, open the door for the mob, and walk due east to the nearest open space. There, think about a holiday honoring whatever interests you, and invite your friends, neighbors, the town alderman, and newspaper reporters over to celebrate.

Suggestions:

Fred's Day
Bonus Friday
Hammock & Lemonade Day
Velvet Underground Appreciation Day
No Underwearensday

83

SECRET #13

Life isn't fair? Fantastic!

As Heraclitus said, "It would not be better if things happened to men just as they wish." Just think, if we magically got whatever we wanted, we'd all be Brad Pitt or Julia Roberts. Imagine a world of 6 billion Brads and Julias driving their 6 billion Mercedes around from one gorgeous palatial mansion to another. The entire planet looking like Beverly Hills meets Fifth Avenue, and not a spot of filth to mar the perfection. Not only that, but the tastiest food is zero calorie, zero carb; your IQ is over 200; your NASDAQ stocks are way, way up. And best of all, every one of the other Brads and Julias really, really loves you and it's just the biggest love fest ever!

If that happened, it would be the end of human struggle. Which would also be the end of progress and new ideas. This process has led us from the cold and darkness of caves to knowing how to make fire to knowing how to illuminate an entire football stadium for night games. Every time in the last 100,000 years that things "went bad," somebody tripped in the dark and decided to make things better. The SuperOptimist knows that when things aren't perfect, it's a sure sign we'll see progress. Every problem is the start of it's own solution!

SECRET #111

Simple visualization for instant upliftment.

At moments of stress, pressure, or bad falls that require hospitalization, a plunge into the mental abyss is not only likely, its probable. It's called "that sinking feeling," and words like quicksand, quagmire, and queasy were invented for just such an occasion. So how can you compensate for being "down in the dumps"?

Close your eyes and visualize your soul as a big wicker laundry basket. Now watch as large hands that look like the opening titles to "Monty Python's Flying Circus" reach down and attach large helium-filled balloons to the basket. The hands disappear, and the basket lifts off from the cellar of hellish misery and goes soaring skyward while the song "Up, Up and Away" by the Fifth Dimension plays. Your soul is floating free, and you might as well join it, because that soul is you, and you are the basket, and everything is beautiful in its own way.

NOTE: *You can repeat this process up to 72 times per day.*

SECRET #27

Notice a pattern here.

Chinese proverb: A little sweat and a lot of laughter each day is good for the soul.

French beauty secret: Sex and laughter slow the aging process.

Cancer survivors: Laughter and doing what you really want lead to miraculous remissions.

So what can we conclude? Lots of sweaty sex and gut-busting laughter would be any reasonable doctor's prescription for a long, happy life. Note the pattern, next determine its benefit, then gladly follow!

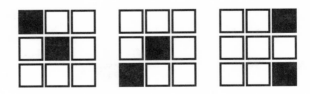

SECRET #69

Whatever you're thinking of charging, add 30%.

People respect expensive. People want to pay more. Add another zero to your fee. They'll thank you for it, and think more of you.

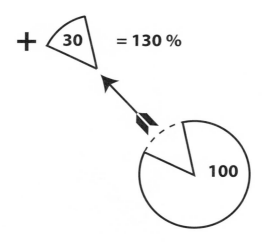

SECRET #17

Whenever you make a purchase, take 70% off.

Haggling isn't just for your friendly Turkish rug sales-man. When purchasing any item other than absolute necessities, ask for 70% off. If the merchant becomes angry, irate, apoplectic, explain to him that you are a SuperOptimist.

NOTE: *If this doesn't work, wait for the 70% off sale.*

SECRET #94

Save the truth for special occasions.

From every perspective –- historical, sociological, cultural, anthropological –- it is proven that the human race doesn't want the truth, enjoy the truth, or is in any way interested in the truth.*

While the SuperOptimist *seeks the truth*, it is also important to experiment with fabrication. Socially, most people prefer a tall tale, an exaggeration, a put-on, a glossy advertisement, a little white lie, a boldfaced lie, a distortion, or fiction disguised as fact -- "You look great in that slimming dress/bold necktie," for instance. The point being, don't be afraid to stretch the truth a little yourself. The SuperOptimist uses dishonesty like Robin Hood used thievery -- to help people feel better, and make life in the woods a lot more fun.

Exception: Journalists who are paid to ferret out the actual truth. Result: Over 60% of the White House Press Corps are on bi-polar or antidepressant medication. (This may not be the exact percentage, but the truth is, we're better off not knowing.)

SECRET #91

Selectively volunteer.

Any former Marine Corps Staff Sergeant with front line experience in combat will tell you the first rule of survival is to avoid volunteering. He knows that whenever any person in a supervisory/command role asks for "volunteers," it means that the job is a dirty, dangerous, and potentially suicidal mission into an uncharted minefield. The same logic applies to most corporate work.

BOSS: "I need a volunteer to work this weekend on the presentation to the client for the new dog food."

BOSS TRANSLATION: "You will work an extra 48 hours in a high-stress desperate attempt to save this poisoned business relationship with a hostile client that is already doomed because of something someone else did, and now we need you as fall guy and in any case there will not be so much as a thank you, because this is a job and we pay you so why should we thank you, anyway?"

NOTE: *The SuperOptimist always volunteers to help those in need, but only as a self-directed choice rather than a submissive response to outside pressures. Volunteering starts on the inside, not the outside.*

SECRET #99

Look for the Gilroy sign.

Most people use the same routes to get from point A to point B. This is the road most travelled, and the sights out the window are familiar. The SuperOptimist doesn't argue that this is a perfectly acceptable way to go, but would point out that the most enlightening stimulus can most likely be found two blocks south.

NOTE: *One of our favorites is CA-152, that takes you from the I-5 to the 101. Look for the "Gilroy" sign.*

SECRET #6

Pennsylvania 6-5000.

Just look around at all the fossils, curmudgeons, and kooks at your cousin's wedding once the band begins to play. You don't need a $45 million government grant to notice that even the most miserable and depressed among us can't help but tap their toes to the great song stylists from the swing era.

So think what happens to a SuperOptimist when he drops a quarter in the jukebox and punches up Bing Crosby, Frank Sinatra, Benny Goodman, Dean Martin, Perry C., Tony B., Peggy Lee. These artists even made lyrics like "Show Me the Way to Get Out of This World" sound as cheery as a daffodil in spring. So "C'mon Get Happy," start shaking to that "Crazy Rhythm," and you'll have "The World on a String" in no time!

NOTE: *In truth, any music that makes you tingle in a good way contributes to SuperOptimism. And let's not forget dancing (Secret #76). That's also good. Except for ballet; it's hard to be SuperOptimistic in overly tight shoes.*

SECRET #33

Losing it is good for you.

Keep a daily notebook of your important thoughts and unique insights. As this notebook builds over time, you'll start to feel it's "really important," it's your "best work," and that somewhere in all your illegible scrawls, there's an idea so wonderful it will be placed alongside Plato, Ovid, and Hemingway as a timeless classic. After you've built this notebook of world-changing beliefs, you should pick a good morning and either:

1) Throw it in a swift-moving river.
2) Leave it on a bus, car, train, or airplane.
3) Burn it in a ceremonial pyre.

Initially you may react: "My God, this is madness!" or "That idea I was having on page 147 -- where a kid runs away from his foster home to join the circus but gets to the big top and learns the clowns are all very sad alcoholic men inside, devoted to muscatel, gambling, and an occasional gruff sexual favor from the bearded lady... my beautiful circus novel is lost!"

The "lost masterpiece" initially feels like a terrible crushing blow, as if a piece of your soul has been destroyed. And the psychic pain resonates, because if it vanished so easily, then you could vanish just as easily.

SECRET #33 - CONTINUED

Why, you're not important at all; just some tiny monkey-bug, crawling in utter darkness!

What the SuperOptimist learns is that he can never, ever lose anything important, because he carries the best ideas inside *at all times*. Loss or destruction of intellectual "property" leads to a new cycle of creation, often with greater clarity and insight. Remember, legend has it that Robert Louis Stevenson's wife, Fanny, threw his first draft of "Dr. Jekyll and Mr. Hyde" into the fire. Stevenson's second draft is the story we cherish today.

EXERCISE: Pick some of your "best" work, and destroy it today!

SECRET #29

Learn to be still for 17 straight hours!

You never know when you'll find yourself in a cramped airline seat, stuck on a runway for an unknown period of time. Or in an elevator, trapped between floors. Or on the highway, after a mud slide closes the expressway during the evening rush.

This type of confined situation can drive even the most rational among us into a state of unmitigated froth -- unless you've learned to be comfortable inside your own head. And if you can do it in an untenable situation, you can do it anywhere.

There are dozens of books, tapes, and classes that can help you with this: zen meditation, yoga, silent prayer -- our favorite technique is counting backwards from 7,919. Spending time inside your own SuperOptimistic skull, quietly watching your own ideas, breath, and the moment itself, can be immensely satisfying. So tune out the bad, turn on the good, and discover that being stuck can be the most enjoyable time of your life. Especially when all those around you are hyperventilating from panic.

SECRET #73

Stop at all rest areas.

Isn't it wonderful that the National Highway System has built rest areas along every stretch of turnpike in America? That's 160,000 miles (256,000 kilometers) of pure possibility. The SuperOptimist takes every opportunity to pull over and take a look around. Last we heard, the most recent verified Bigfoot sighting in the state of Oregon was at a rest area off the I-5 north of Medford. Don't forget your camera.

And if you did forget your camera at that one unique moment, there is no downside. You can still take an even more important "mental picture" -- that no one else can.

SECRET #49

More is less.

First-world nations are now living in a state of science fiction that only the most prescient of futurists predicted a short time ago. Today, people are called "consumers" rather than "humans," and judged more on their spending behavior than on their self-knowledge or individualism.

The culprit? Savvy marketers who target all 4 trillion cells in your body.* Using the pseudo-science of "Focus Groups," they invent messages that create gaping holes in your cell lining. Once they determine where a hole may exist, they work feverishly to program a message that causes your Automatic Reach Mechanism (ARM) to switch "on" and your common sense to switch "off." A purchase will immediately fill the hole, but almost instantly your cells will dissolve the purchase with acid reflux and more holes will be created.

When you feel a "want," use your SuperOptimist mindset to turn away from a purchase, and towards productivity. The more you produce, the less you'll consume.

* Approximation; cells are tiny - ten more cell divisions could change this number by millions and it's hard to measure accurately in any case.

SECRET #43

Can too.

How many times do we say "I can't" in a lifetime? A thousand? Ten thousand? Try adding a few zeros to that! We start when we're young, as a way to control our parents and get them to do things for us that prove difficult. "I can't tie my shoes." "I can't eat anymore lima beans." "I can't go poopy." In high school, it becomes: "I can't ask her out." "I can't do trigonometry." "I can't run the 440 in under 23 seconds." Then later, in adulthood, we continue the self-defeating mantra, only this time, it's "I can't finish by Tuesday." "I can't ask for a raise." "I can't tell my spouse I don't love him anymore and want to live in a small grass hut with the handyman." What seems innocent enough when we're little, creates a self-fulfilling prophecy as we age. "I can't" becomes a shield of social inadequacy to protect us from perceived dangers, or embarrassments, or (especially) hard work.

Guess what? *You actually can*! Granted it might be frightening at first to admit that a lot of your "can'ts" are just excuses. But the SuperOptimist seizes this as another opportunity for re-dialog. Remove the words "I can't" from your vocabulary. A whole new world will open up to you -- starting with that skydiving lesson you've been putting off. Try this new dialog on for size: *"I can, and right now!"*

SECRET #40

Run towards what scares you.

Snakes? Heights? Enclosed spaces? Your mother-in-law? Open your arms and make a beeline to the source of your fear. Embrace it, squeeze it, and you'll realize that your anxiety was unfounded. At worst, you'll get in some trouble and learn a valuable lesson. But at least you confronted it! And that's worth more than you know.

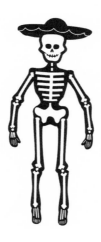

Let's take a lesson from old Mexico's Day of the Dead. Rather than fearing the reaper, it's a chance to joyfully celebrate departed ancestors. (November 1 & 2.)

SECRET #47

Have interesting answer to questions, even if you have to make them up.

The most asked question of adults is the classic "What do you do for a living?" You could go with the conventional "lawyer" or "accountant" or "high school driving instructor" and see the glaze come over your questioner's eyes. Instead, try one of the following replies:

1. Sherpa of plenitude
2. Anesthesiologist
3. USTA certified tennis instructor
4. Fifth member of the Fantastic Four
5. Swami
6. Artist of dishwashing
7. Artist of small engine repair
8. Glider pilot
9. Seeker of beauty in a job that others deem unworthy

Soon, with very little practice, the SuperOptimist learns an amazing fact: Most people don't even listen to your answers to their questions. Try it, you'll see!

SECRET #103

Woof!

You'll never truly understand the nature of happiness and trust that can exist between two beings until you've become a dog owner. Dogs can't talk but their extreme social orientation to humans will give you insights into animal and human behaviors. There are also the Zen-like pleasures of chewed shoes, stained and damaged carpets, and other reminders not to be attached to materialism or schedules. And let's not forget the humble "service tasks" of feeding, combing, and waste cleanup. Payback? If you are a good dog owner, you receive pure distilled love and devotion so overwhelming, you are sure to say "sit!" and "down!"

To a dog, shoe leather and the yummy rawhide pet chew-toy taste exactly the same. Mmmm.

SECRET #71

Ahoy, Captain.

Your yacht needs a name. You read that correctly. Your yacht. You're a SuperOptimist, aren't you? So you might as well be prepared for your inevitable success. Here are some possible names to get you started:

Black Betty
The Sock Puppet
Love Sink
Godot
La Agua Chorizo

NOTE: *This secret hinges on the hidden power of naming objects. The instant anything is named, it becomes much more real in the mind. Choose names carefully and you'll leverage this vital force to your cause.*

SECRET #100

Two eyes? Count again.

When the daily routine numbs the mind's edges and everything seems too familiar, that's the signal for you to crack open your *l'oie troisieme,* or third eye.

The third eye (in medical terminology, the pineal gland) is a peanut-sized organ at the exact center of your brain. The third eye has long been considered by mystics and spiritual adepts to be the seat of potential psychic powers. It acts as a sensitive two-way radio, by which vibrations of many different types can be translated, interpreted, and dispersed to gain wisdom and illumination. Through this eye, higher entities are perceived, and it may be the basis of our everyday feelings of "intuition."

SuperOptimists gain an immediate sense of empowerment by the simple act of realizing that they do not have two eyes, but three. This can be as good as finding out you have 33% more cash in the bank or an extra wheel for your bicycle. Know and remind yourself that you have an extra special eye and who knows what you might sense!

SECRET #6

Here comes Mabel.

A Floridian friend lost all her worldly possessions in a recent hurricane. Her small houseboat was crushed and she found herself running for her life. In spite of her tremendous loss, several days later she surveyed the destruction around her and thought, "How fortunate. I've been given a gift few people ever get. I get to be reborn. I get to completely start my life over."

Are you prepared to lose everything and maintain an optimistic attitude? Will it take a tsunami to get you to clean house? Will it take a tornado to get you to throw out your old underwear? We suggest that you use this moment to give away, donate, or otherwise divest yourself of three (3) items you own right now. This "loss" will immediately become a "gain." Why not stop reading and do this now. We'll meet you back here.

NOTE: *The SuperOptimist is aware that hurricanes are given pleasant names like "Isabel" and "Henry" because they are really our friends in helping us "clean house" and get to the next plateau!*

SECRET #63

There is no "Plan B".

Frequently, you'll hear someone say: "And if that doesn't work -- we'll proceed to Plan B."

This is just "planning for failure." The SuperOptimist is of the mind that all energy down to our very last molecule should be focused on achieving the primary goal -- and that any time spent planning for failure, setbacks, or humbling defeat only activates fear. Fear that Plan A won't work. Fear that something may go wrong. When other people sense that you doubt your course, they, too, become afraid.

Imagine you're a passenger in an airplane and the captain comes on the intercom and says: "We'll be landing soon at O'Hare International Airport -- unless I can't get the wheels down -- and if that's the case we'll go to Plan B." Nobody really wants to hear someone say that. The SuperOptimist conclusion: any Plan "A" is superior to every Plan "B."

NOTE: If you don't have a "Plan A," go get a darn good one. With a solid plan, karmic forces will line up behind you and see that you have good luck on your side. We're with you.

SECRET #10.3

Fired? Displaced? Lucky you.

There's nothing quite like waking up in the morning and finding a sign in front of your rented dwelling that says "For Sale." Some people would become upset at the callous landlord who failed to tip off the tenant that there's a "change in the works;" namely, the former renter's imminent displacement to the street. But in more practical terms, this is a fine chance for all-new developments that could be very interesting. Get out of your box. Also, it's a reminder that nothing you see is permanent; everything wonderful just bubbles up out of uncreated time.

Each forced move from home or job, sudden firing, psychological beating, dietary mistake, and broken promise is but a stroke of the paddle in life's canoe. Try to remember there's no point in getting in a canoe if you're unwilling to get wet. Focus on the journey, not the water-logged shoes. Why, if you're really lucky, you may even see a frog before they're all gone.

SECRET #24.1

Woe is just eow spelled backwards.

The next time you're feeling dyspeptic, try spelling it backwards. That's "citpepsyd," which is odd, because that's darn near a brand name of antacid. With "cit" in front of it. Which is a big insurance brokerage, if we're not mistaken. Which means you're feeling an insurance antacid, which is rather funny when you think about it. And by the time you've done all that in your head, you probably won't remember you're dyspeptic any longer. All you'll really feel is smug that you figured out where that famous antacid got its name.

Want another one? Pain is "niap." What's niap? "I'm in a lot of niap right now?" That sounds silly. And silly is good. It's a lot better than pain, that's for sure.

Oh, no, I'm having an anxiety attack. Backwards, I'm having an yteixna kcatta, which I can't even pronounce. So it's nothing, I'm having nothing, which is good.

Turn it around, and it won't be able to turn around on you. YakO? (That's "Okay" spelled backwards, in case you were wondering.)

SECRET #45.7

Put on your happy pie.

It's a documented fact that during the seasons known as fall and winter, the decreased amount of sunlight can lead some people to feel down, dopey, and lethargic. It's called "Seasonal Affective Disorder," or SAD. What's not known to many SAD sufferers is a readily available antidote that can relieve many of their symptoms. And that is to jump out of bed, run out the door, and get some *pie*. Eating pie has the unique ability to distract you from the demons of darkness who come knocking at your chamber door. Pie also goes great with coffee, yessir. There are literally hundreds of pies to bake and eat: here's a short list to get your mouth watering:

Apple pie
Cherry pie
Banana cream pie
Pumpkin Gingersnap pie
Rhubarb Meringue pie
White Russian pie

NOTE: *Alternatively, to lift your spirits, you can always take a whole pie and throw it at someone, preferably a politician who's not telling us the truth about his relationship with the military-industrial complex.*

SECRET #44.4

Respect the pineapple.

Nothing says *"You're welcome here!"* like a pineapple --
without question the most historically valid symbol of
hospitality of any fruit or vegetable.

The first account of the pineapple was given by Christo-
pher Columbus and his men, who landed on the island
now known as Guadeloupe on their second voyage of
discovery. One of the first things they saw was a pineapple (though they had no name for it).

Columbus brought the succulent fruit back to Europe
in 1493. Its cylindrical shape and rough, spiky surface
caused the Spaniards to name it "pina," after the pine
cone, although the pineapple is much larger by comparison. The English noted the same resemblance, but
also liked apples, hence the word "pineapple."

Spaniards began placing a pineapple at the entrance to
a village as a sign of welcome. This symbolism spread to
Europe, then to Colonial North America, where families
would set a fresh pineapple in the middle of the table as
a colorful centerpiece, especially when visitors joined
them in celebration. The fruit would then be served as
a special desert after the meal. Often when the visitor
spent the night, he was given the bedroom which had
pineapples intricately carved on the bedposts or atop

the headboard -- even if the bedroom belonged to the head of the household. Thus the phrase "I slept with the pineapples" means getting a good night's rest.

WELCOME

The pineapple is the leading edible member of the family Bromeliaceae which embraces about 2,000 species, mostly epiphytic and many strikingly ornamental. Now known botanically as Ananas comosus Merr. (syns. A. sativus Schult. f., Ananassa sativa Lindl., Bromelia ananas L., B. comosa L)

SECRET #21.8

Seek new information.

One key to living well is to remain teachable. There is nothing wrong with expressing a need for new information or assistance to clear your fogged-in head. In fact, why not go out and find yourself a trustworthy teacher in any field, and completely open yourself up to a new batch of knowledge heretofore unknown to you. While wise oracles have noted that learning is a life-long activity, the SuperOptimist knows it's not simply experiencing the shock of the new (good) but also the "what" you pick to study. Rather than choose to learn practical things like how to speak Spanish, you might get far more out of studying something less obvious. Here are a few proven class suggestions to get you started, each guaranteed to activate unexplored regions of your brain.

old-time banjo
open-pit BBQ cooking
nude-life drawing
dirt-bike riding
French physicist Blaise Pascal

SECRET #52.4

Beware greed in yourself.
Study it in others.

Whenever you find yourself irritable, restless, un-nerved, constipated, or madder than hell, the forces of envy and jealousy are usually the culprits. The wanton pursuit of something you don't have can send you to the nut house if you're not careful. Boob jobs, stock manipulation, political lobbying, plagiarism, and teen-idol worship are just a few cases where blatant disregard for one's own blessings leads to a pell-mell hustle for a materialistic boost. One universal example comes from a family gathered to watch their mother pass on. They could either selflessly give their time to helping their poor mom enjoy her last days on earth. Or start quibbling about how much they deserve of her possessions before she's even died. This *Treasure of the Sierra Madre* scenario happens every day -- in boardrooms, bedrooms, and electronics stores all over the world. So watch yourself, or you may wind up holding an empty bag of dust instead of millions worth of gold. Without the right attitude, the gold's worthless anyhow!

SECRET #15.5

Wear a T-shirt with your own brand name on it.

The past half century has seen the rise of an interesting phenomenon -- an individual will actually pay a corporation to wear the company's logo on their chest, head, wrists, legs, or feet, sometimes all at once. The billion-dollar behemoth not only gets your hard-earned cash, they get free advertising! What science may yet determine is that by doing so, we are actually sublimating our own personalities and unconsciously taking on the properties of a FORTUNE 500 company. Considering the types of people at the tops of these giant Ponzi schemes, this can't be good for our health and well-being. The SuperOptimist suggestion: print up some clothing with your own name on it. Not only will this remind others of who you are, but you'll never again have to wear those annoying *Hello, my name is* stickers at a conference or high school reunion. Plus you might end up starting a fashion trend and become a tres chic Seventh Avenue label.

SECRET #8.6

Go for the real butter.

Back in the days of the medieval village, a group of farmers and craftsmen produced an estimated 23 items, including beefsteak, lettuce, wheat, shoes, beer, wine, rope, cheese, and candles. In contrast, the postmodern supermarket/pharmacy/discount store offers as many as 17,800 products -- most with names like WHIZZO! or PUFT! or FREEDLES! These modern items are, in fact, mere substitutions for the "real" items that were produced by the caring crafters of ye olde village. Do we really believe that anyone has invented a substitute that tastes better than butter? Read the label of the "new and improved" brands. You'll find that most things today are actually made of this:

TYPICAL INGREDIENTS:
Beef tallow, corn syrup extract, maltodextrin, modified food starch, 100% refined sugar, unextracted corn syrup, salt, beet sugar, and salt.

The SuperOptimist knows "real" items are 93% better-tasting compared to simulated replacements. What's more, they usually cost less and are healthier for you.

Hint: real foods are often just one color.

SECRET #0.1

Forget it.

Humans are "memetic." They repeat what they see and hear. If humans didn't love repeating patterns we would not have language, music, crossword puzzles, or very complicated highway systems with numbers and letters to identify them, e.g. I-80, 405N, etc.

What's a SuperOptimist to think about repeating old patterns and mistakes? You should not criticize yourself for returning to the familiar, to sample "what you know." But more important is to exist primarily in this present moment. As long as you are recognizing your own behavior now, this minute, and are conscious of what you are doing, you are on the right road. Is the rudder on your personal cruise ship navigating the "Momentary Now?"

For the purposes of this exercise, we'll concentrate on just staying in the present. Just sit in a chair and stare at something for 5 minutes. A flower. A rock. If during this period you happen to recall anything unpleasant from your past, simply say to yourself: "forget it, that's the old me. I'm the new me."

SECRET #11.3

Subvert authority.
Start your own publishing company.

Why not? Ben Franklin did. So did Mark Twain. And Walt Whitman. In fact, here's a SuperOptimist secret: a world-renowned publisher purchased this book and agreed to distribute it by the thousands. But as soon as the waterproof ink was dry on their specious contract, they tried to distort the essential truth of this philosophical treatise to the point that it was essentially unrecognizable. Rather than take the money and run, the transmitters bought the rights back from the publisher and printed it themselves.

It is always more important to disseminate your own work as it stands than to allow robot monkeys in a corporate office park to micromanage, repackage, and nullify its soul. Do it yourself. Make something. You'll be glad you did and you'll amaze your friends.

SECRET #3.4

It's an inside job.

The most successful safecrackers, bank robbers, jewel thieves, business tycoons, stock manipulators, actors, and prostitutes agree: success is more likely if it's an inside job. The shamanist rituals of self-produced ecstasy apply here: happiness conjured from within. No externals are needed; not a single one. A guide? There are plenty, but we suggest reading, writing, and meditating your way to a better world. The more you practice, the more you'll gain access to your own orgiastic enclave no matter where you may find yourself. Including bus stations with loud children, business conference rooms where the meeting is not going well, and hostile French bistros, to name but a few.

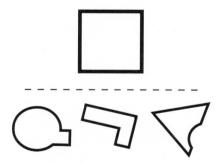

What two shapes can fit inside this box exactly?

SECRET #84.1

Whatever your parents told you, do the opposite.

Your parents meant well. Or maybe they didn't. Whatever the case, the dogma they fed you about religion, quality schooling, secure career paths, moderated drug intake, and limited sexual intercourse was from a position of fear and control. No doubt they did all the things they are now telling you not to do. (Or even if they didn't, they wanted to, but were too afraid thanks to what their parents told them.)

Obviously, turning your back on a blue-chip law degree in favor of playing the electric saw in a post-apocalyptic bluegrass band may not seem to make sense, at least not to your mother and dad, and maybe not to your friends or other loved ones either. But by high-tailing it in *the opposite direction of safe,* you'll get a chance to find out for yourself about where the limits are. And it could be there are no limits at all! Wouldn't that be nice? This kind of character-building exercise in removing all restraint is invaluable, and can't be found in the glossy color catalog of any four-year college, as far as we know. Are you listening, Amherst?

SECRET #2.6

Take advantage of
free electrical outlets.

A former Fortune 500 CEO now spends his time parked at the beach in his RV, watching Hi-Def telemundo soccer while plugged into the Los Angeles municipal power grid. He's powered by "free." We can all take note of his example.

Be on the lookout for wi-fi hotspots, complimentary breakfasts at hotels, and goodie bags at trendy parties. There's a lot of free stuff in the world ranging from the really tremendous -- air, sunsets, and green grass -- to the more mundane, like concert ticket giveaways, free iPod promotions, vacations for those willing to listen to a time-share pitch, bus tickets to Vegas, and so much more. An Ohio SuperOptimist reports living "free and clear" for the last seven years exclusively from the swag he gained by jumping on every freebie contest, sweepstakes, raffle, party, art opening, and "free to anyone with a truck --you pick up" posting. Once you start living the good life *gratis*, you'll wonder why you ever slaved twelve hours a day at a thankless job just to buy a toaster oven that broke the third time you used it.

NOTE: many stores offer free samples. Just ask.

SECRET #9.6

Believe in something big.

If you have faith, use it. Faith in your God, or other very powerful spiritual beings, (i.e. elves, fairies, trolls, unicorns, aliens, talking dragons, etc.) is very helpful to many of us. Whatever (**X**) you choose to believe in, stick with it and don't be wishy-washy. The SuperOptimist knows there is huge value in the ability to:

A) believe in some (**X**) that's really big and powerful.

B) believe the big powerful (**X**) is on "your team."

C) believe big powerful (**X**) will bail you out when you get in over your head in some crazy situation you never would have gotten into in the first place if you didn't think you had (**X**) on your side.

NOTE: The best thing about faith is that it's free! And you can have as much as you can carry with you, and even if you carry a very large amount of faith in something very big, it does not necessarily need to weigh you down.

ADDENDUM

fig. 1:

Architectural plan for the proposed Institute for SuperOptimism

(Hannibal, Missouri)

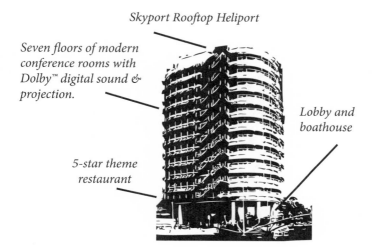

Skyport Rooftop Heliport

Seven floors of modern
conference rooms with
Dolby™ digital sound &
projection.

Lobby and
boathouse

5-star theme
restaurant

Based on the success of Dubai City in the United Arab Emirates, a team of SuperOptimists have proposed a visionary project of similar proportions on the banks of the Mississippi in America's heartland. If global fund-raising continues at its current pace, we expect to break ground on this center for modern learning in the very near future. Watch for announcements.

EXERCISE 1:

The SuperOptimal Diet.

The SuperOptimist takes nothing for granted, including the amount of time one is accorded on Planet Earth. You might have another 50 years to live, or today might be bye-bye. You never know. So while diet is an important regimen for staying fit and feeling good, we do not advocate picking at sprouts and tofu while hungrily eyeing the plate of quesadillas at the table next to you. Would you want two slices of whole wheat toast (dry) and egg whites to be your last meal? Don't be a glutton, just eat what makes you feel good, mix it up, and savor every bite! Among our list of SuperOpt foods:

Broccoli
Tomatoes
Blackberries
Cheesesteak
Curly fries
Ice cream soda

EXERCISE 2:

Your Invisible Force Shield.

This may sound like an invention from a Hollywood animation department. But remember: to create a fantasy, it has to exist in the mind first! So how can you harness the same powers that superheroes have? How can you become untouchable by negative forces, impenetrable to blame, problems, and strife? With your mind, and the invisible force shield it conjures up!

It all starts by believing you have one.

Minor irritations bounce off it. Small mistakes can't penetrate it. Ridiculous bosses can't dismantle it. Start your day by holding it in front of you as you walk to work or out the window as you drive your car. It's your Force Shield; you can project it anywhere you want.

EXERCISE 3:

Your Invention Here.

Already in life there are objects and inventions that are implicitly and automatically SuperOptimistic in their very nature. We'll give you a head start with a few items; see what you can add to this list:

Zero gravity
Wire cutters
No money down
Laughing gas
teflon
lemonade
all you can eat shrimp
life after death
exit strategies
bulletproof vest
medicine ball
gum

EXERCISE 4:

Visual Acuity Test.

When you look at this picture, what do you see?

NOTE: *there are no wrong answers.*

EXERCISE 5:

Study Another Culture.

Sample profile - The Danes

A recent values survey reveals that the most satisfied citizens in the world are the joyful Danes. Almost 100 percent of Danish people reported being contented with their lives. One reason: the citizens of Denmark have a healthy disrespect for authority in any form, and this makes for independent thought and action in every area of life. Also, unlike many other countries, the Danes generally disapprove of cheating, bribery, and lying for one's own benefit. In fact, Scandinavians in general frown upon people betraying the social trust. Finally, let's not forget they've given us some of the world's best painters, artists, musicians, thinkers, and most importantly, Danish pastry. Here's to the Danes: SuperOptimists by nature!

EXERCISE 6:

Essential Memory Work.

Think of a wonderful sexual experience you've had. Remember all the salient details of how great it was and what an unbelievable lover you are. Write about the experience as a short letter -- *from the other person to you* -- complimenting you on just how good you were, and mail it to yourself. We'll start you off with the sample letter below and you can complete the full exercise on your own.

Dearest (Your Name),

I don't think I've ever experienced pleasure as great as the incandescent joy I felt when you kissed me. I must say that of all the people who have lived through all the ages of eternity and back, you are, for me, the greatest lover I can ever possibly imagine. I can barely tell you -- but I will -- how exciting it was when you touched my hot and ready _____...

Suggested Length: 30 minutes, 250 words.

EXERCISE 7:

Mathematical Income Verification.

How much money do you really need? To live in the capital of capitalism, it is nearly impossible to not think of money as essential. Yet chasing cash causes us to grey prematurely, become stiff and unlovable, and die without ever having truly lived. Consider the paradox that Xenodotus of Athens (4th century B.C.) called "the painful arrows of time." Just when it seems like you should have a lot more, you in fact have far less.

Xenodotus' arrows: the upside is the downside.

For a better way to look at money, try the following: if you have $1 to your name, you have more than the person who has nothing. If you have $10, you have more than the person who has $1, plus the person who has nothing. If you have $100, you have still more than the person who has $10, $1, and nothing. And so on. Write down on a piece of paper the total you have (approximate). Do you now have more than before or not?

EXERCISE 8:

Fun With Words.

Add the following to your vocabulary and experience immediate serotonin reuptake.

1. Transcendent
2. Ventriloquism
3. Isometrics
4. Opportunity
5. Shoeshine
6. Truce
7. Self-employed
8. Detachment
9. Osprey

Alternative: *Beekeeper*

EXERCISE 9:

Modern Potlatch Time.

Many ancient traditions provide profound health and wellness benefits for us today. For example: yoga, Zen meditation, climbing stairs rather than taking either the escalator or the elevator.

Now, for a change of pace, why not have a "potlatch."

Among North American Indians, gift-giving was a central feature of social life. The tribes of the Pacific Northwest and Canada went a step further. Those hosting a potlatch would give away all their wealth and material possesions to show goodwill to the rest of the tribe and to solidify their social status.

How it's done:

Just give away all your worldly possessions to people around you. This undercuts taxes, laws, inheritance, and even removes the usual idea of ownership. Don't hold back. The more you give away, the more you'll get back in the form of thanks, hugs, attention, and good will.

Fig. 18. Sioux Indian teepee (tipi) and an ultra-modern condominium. Have we made true progress in how to live happier lives or just gotten more square?

NOTE: *Canadian law prohibited the potlatch in 1884. Luckily, with the U.S. passage of the Indian Reorganization Act of 1934 and the Canadian Indian Act of 1951, the potlatch was resumed legally. It remains a central feature of Pacific Northwest Indian life today. It is also legal for you -- since the law does not mandate you be an Indian -- to potlatch!*

EXERCISE #10:

Life-affirming ways of looking at the unexpected death of a close friend or relative.

Often, we're caught "off guard" by hearing about death, and in that moment are overwhelmed with pain and loss and grief. It's never too soon to get back on the SuperOptimal track with the following thoughts about the recently departed:

1. He or she can't feel any pain, and that's a blessing. If they can't feel pain anymore, how does it make any sense for me to feel pain? (It doesn't.)
2. I'm damned lucky it wasn't me. Lucky for now.
3. We're all gonna die, so I might as well make this a great day while I'm still here.
4. Sure I feel sad, who wouldn't? But I don't have to crawl in the hole with them. That's no fun.
5. He/She lived _____ years. Some people are never even born.
6. It could have been worse, I guess. Actually, I'm sure.
7. I'm not a wizard, so there's nothing I can do.
8. If we don't inform the government, they may keep sending the social security check for quite awhile.

Life? Death? Beauty? Ugly?
All just a matter of perspective.

EXERCISE #11:

Take tiny powerful steps.

Focus on your achievements no matter how small. Set miniscule goals that are attainable and reward yourself when you achieve each step. Nobody gets there in one giant leap -- it takes time and effort to achieve anything. The SuperOptimist knows that if you are not achieving your goals, the easy and almost impossibly powerful one-step solution is to make your goals smaller. That's so important we're going to repeat it, right here: Take smaller steps. The smaller the better. Even taking no step at all may be the place you need to start.

EXERCISE: Repeat this phrase 2x aloud: I won't do it all right now. I won't try to. I will do 1/4 of everything and that will be plenty. I can stop at any time to play a board game or eat some fruit.

EXERCISE #12:

Imagine it done "your way."

Now, while some writers, artists, inventors, craftsmen, and pessimists get paralyzed by the idea of: "It's all been done before," thinking like that is actually an avenue to SuperOptimal power. Rather than having to start from scratch, you can take something that already exists and imagine a few slight improvements that will turn it into "your version."

In this exercise, practice imagining something "big." For example, The Golden Gate Bridge. Instead of that familiar deep red, what if yours was painted in a gleaming metallic silver? Classy! Or a vibrant sunny yellow? Energized! Once you've applied this idea to a few of the titanic and loved accomplishments of mankind, you'll see that there is no reason you shouldn't have a seat at the "big table."

EXERCISE 13:

Cut and Carry

If you lose track of where you are in the 8 stages of SuperOptimism, this pocket reminder card may help you get back on track.

```
S.O. STAGES

1. Pain, horror, shock, loss, suffering, and a
world of hurt.

2. Complete calm and quiet self-observa-
tion.

3. Reframing the situation from the S.O. per-
spective.

4. Re-booting the brain.

5. Re-engagement with the world.

6. Awakened attention.

7. Complete joy, bliss, and success beyond all
expectation.

8. Return to step 1, with practice, you can
jump to step 3.
```

EXCURSUS

APPENDIX I

The worst that can happen:
A SuperOptimal Checklist.

Here's your easy-to-remember one page checklist of worst fears and corresponding SuperOptimist solutions. Perfect for purse, wallet, or breast pocket. Lamination advised before laundering clothes.

1. DEATH. Since no one's absolutely positive about what's on the other side of the curtain, there's at least a 50% chance that there is, in fact, a better life waiting for you after this one.

2. HOMELESSNESS. All your responsibilities are removed! You're off the grid and the living is easy. Move to a warm climate.

3. JAIL. Opportunities abound -- getting sober, writing fiction, getting a college education, even achieving a law degree so you can fire your court appointed attorney and plead your own case.

4. INSANITY. Apply your madness and you could become a great artist. The French even have a term for it: *L'art chez les fous.* Collectors pay big money for art by those judged completely insane at one point or another.

APPENDIX II

Inner Shaman Practicum.

While admittedly not everyone is cut out to be a seer, spirit channel, or voyager to higher levels of reality, we do encourage readers to experiment with wearing a mask. This ancient activity allows humans to access their true identity, superego, and true self. Moreover, 1 person out of every 362 has the potential to become an activated spirit-channel. Maybe it's you!

INSTRUCTIONS: The reverse side of this page can be torn out and/or photocopied and placed over the eyes. Go look at yourself in the mirror. Is it still you? If not, who? Ideally, you will be transported from your current state of reality and have a mystical experience. If not, be patient and try again. You are also invited to conceive a more personalized mask based on an animal motif or other natural spirit-guide. Enjoy!

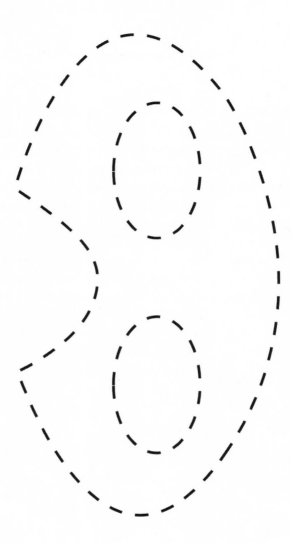

APPENDIX III

Shaman Practicum II:
personal perspective & field report.

Right now, I am wearing a spotted yellow kitten mask. I have been wearing it for 72 hours straight. It makes typing rather difficult, and knocks out my peripheral vision. Yet it is indispensable to my work at the present time. Why? Because it frees me from the identity of man at computer with deadline and little motivation to one of catlike intuition, feline wiles, and furry fun. Upon donning the mask, my vague unease and mid-afternoon slump change and I am suddenly light on my feet, even though I am sitting in a chair. I lick my fingernails and purr, two activities I don't normally incorporate into my daily routine. I also may go up on the roof and leap off, just to see if this nine lives business is true. So why does the simple act of covering my face with a sliver of foam rubber have such transformative power?

1. Wearing a mask is an ancient practice that enables any human to transcend the shackles of ingrained behavior.

2. They've been used since the Stone Age so there must be something to it.

3. It triggers a trancelike state as the wearer assumes the spirit character depicted by the mask.

I urge you to try any one of the mundane activities which fill up your day while wearing a mask and experience the difference. Any mask will do: Zorro, Mardi Gras, African tribal, "Presidential" rubber. Put it on before your morning commute and see what happens. Riding on the train, you'll feel a surge of excitement behind your mask, as if you were having an out-of-body experience distinct from all the other habitual Wall Street Journal readers, whose uncomfortable sidelong glances just feed your sense of playful adventure. At work, you'll receive laughter from your coworkers and a visit from the lady in Human Resources, but also a newfound respect in your willingness to deviate from the norm. And despite their pleas to take the "crazy" mask off, don't. Hold your ground and see the mob for what they are: scared, nervous, wishing they could cross the invisible line and wear a mask like you!

Masks. What kind are you wearing now?

APPENDIX IV

Official slogan.

At the recent International Council of SuperOptimists meeting (ICoS) which took place in Calgary, Canada, a new all-purpose slogan was adopted as the official mantra for the next 100 years:

"I can handle it!"

The phrase "I can handle it!" is exactly the kind of thing SuperOptimists like to hear in the event of:

1) car crash
2) hostile divorce
3) nuclear incident
4) spoiled milk
5) dog mess on rug
6) avian flu
7) tooth pain
8) flab
8a) more flab

9) terrorist incursions
10) stinky kitty box
11) bad political leadership
12) another meeting at work
13) laundry problems
14) parking ticket
15) computer virus
16) impulse control problem
17) _____ (insert your issue here)

SECRETS OF THE SUPEROPTIMIST

APPENDIX IV

Escape from hunter-gatherer hell.

Let's take a historical perspective. Today, you probably wonder why you have all the bric-a-brac around the house. It's because 100,000 years ago your ancestors learned that they had better gather as many nuts as possible, or they'd starve during the Ice Age.

What happened over the next 100 centuries? As the cave dwellers caught wild beasts and fought the stormy elements (basically participating in a giant 3-D action movie, but without Bruce Willis), their brains learned that there was a "rush" of pleasure associated with the risk-reward cycle.

Now repeat that process a million times over 100,000 years. What happens is that you evolve into strange creatures like us. Animals that like to keep running on the wheel after the low hanging fruit, overextending, clawing and climbing for the next pay raise. The new car. The tassled loafers. We continue eating food we know is bad for us. We drink and smoke things we know will kill us.

Our brains hunger to repeat sensations we remember as being intensely pleasurable (whether they still are or not). This is nature's trick, one we must recognize.

The SuperOptimist knows that armed with this evolving historical perspective on how we all became such uber-consumers over 100,000 years, that there is an easy solution to beating nature at this trick. And that answer: Enjoy the old.

That's right. While it's possible to find pleasure in the new, it is also possible to find it in the old, the used, the worn. Love your deep-set wrinkles! Think of the Antiques Roadshow! Realize that you are becoming a priceless one-of-a-kind antique.

PASS IT ON.

The SuperOptimist has communicated with humanity to help you help you. That's right, to *help you help you* (note: repetition is a key ingredient to absorbing these secrets and putting them to work in your daily life). In addition, you are encouraged to spread the word and help the people around you. In the spirit of giving, it is suggested that you pass this book on to someone you believe could benefit from becoming 9 to 12 times more optimistic. Better yet, offer it to a complete stranger. The results will be outstanding!

ABOUT THE TRANSMITTERS.

W. R. Morton and Nathaniel Whitten have been seek-
ers of higher truth and optimal sensation for more than
3 decades. Since their encounter with the SuperOptimist, they've made it their mission to pass along this
vital information to all who wish to receive it. Indi-
vidually and collectively, they have studied shamanistic
meta-psychology, Zen, wabi-sabi, neuro-muscular sciences, healing arts, traditional kung fu, tai chi, literary
deconstruction, and various foreign languages.

They can be contacted for one-on-one consultations or
corporate wellness seminars at The Institute for Super-
Optimism headquarters in Venice, CA.

www.superoptimist.com

A NOTE ON THE TYPE

This book is set in Minion Pro, a typeface designed by Robert Slimbach. Minion Pro is inspired by classical typefaces of the late Renaissance, a period of elegant, beautiful, and highly readable type designs. Minion Pro combines the aesthetic and functional qualities that make text type highly readable with the versatility of a full alphabet of twenty-six letters, plus other signs, symbols, marks and glyphs that remain a mystery. For example, this weird thing: ð

This page unintentionally left blank.